CFDs

The Definitive Guide to Contracts for Difference

by David James Norman

HARRIMAN HOUSE LTD

3A Penns Road
Petersfield
Hampshire
GU32 2EW
GREAT BRITAIN

Tel: +44 (0)1730 233870
Fax: +44 (0)1730 233880
Email: enquiries@harriman-house.com
Website: www.harriman-house.com

First published in Great Britain in 2009

Copyright © Harriman House Ltd

The right of David James Norman to be identified as the author has been asserted
in accordance with the Copyright, Design and Patents Act 1988.

ISBN 978-1-905641-43-7

British Library Cataloguing in Publication Data
A CIP catalogue record for this book can be obtained from the British Library.

Printed and bound by CPI Antony Rowe, Chippenham.

Designated trademarks and brands are the property of their respective owners.

Contents

About the Author

David James Norman has been teaching and writing about market technology and trading for over 20 years. He teaches regular courses in market data, algorithmics, intermarket trading strategies and CFDs, and heads the teaching faculty at The Trader Training Company.

He is the author of four books on trading and market technology: *Trading at the Speed of Light* (Paradym, 2001), *Professional Electronic Trading* (John Wiley & Sons, 2002), *Trader DNA* (Paradym, 2006) and *The Little Book of Trading Wisdom* (O4MT, 2009).

Preface

Who this book is for

The book has been written for anyone who is interested in CFDs either from a trading, broking, regulatory, or IT viewpoint, as a current user of the product, or as a newcomer.

With regard to trading the book aims to provide CFD traders of all experience levels with further knowledge of how to maximise trading opportunities and improve the effectiveness of CFD trading strategies. The book will also describe the growing range of cash instruments that CFDs are linked to.

Regulators, exchange staff, lawyers and financial markets consultants may also find the text useful with regard to the principals and mechanics of CFD trading, as well as the product definitions, the money flows and the treatment of risk.

While a grasp of CFD terminology and some familiarity with the product would be useful, they are not a prerequisite for understanding the key concepts in the book.

What the book covers

In recent years, CFDs have become the favoured trading instrument for a range of market participants. As primary derivatives of a broad range of cash instruments – including stocks, commodities, currencies, stock indices and bonds – CFDs offer flexibility, leverage and cost-effective trading opportunities to institutional, professional and non-professional traders alike.

The book covers the following topics:

- What CFDs are
- The range of CFD products available
- How a CFD is priced
- The mechanics of opening, funding and maintaining a CFD trading account and the different types of account that are available

- The logistics of trading CFDs, including details of the tradable markets, underlying instruments and strategies
- The benefits and risks of trading CFDs, including leverage, shorting and hedging
- A comparison between CFDs and other trading instruments such as spread betting, covered warrants and cash equities
- The ways in which CFDs can be accessed via different providers, including direct electronic market access facilities, broker intermediation and market maker quoting mechanisms
- A range of CFD trading strategies for different market conditions
- A description of money management and risk control methods through the use of stop loss limits, guaranteed stops and limited liability orders
- Current CFD regulatory issues and expectations for the future of the industry

Note

The first CFDs were equity related. Since then the range of CFDs has grown hugely, such that today there are CFDs on equities, indices, bonds, commodities, forex and other instruments. However, the CFD market is still dominated by equities and for that reason this book focuses on equities, although the information is in almost all cases equally applicable to the other instruments.

How the book is structured

The book has six main parts:

1. The principles of CFDs
2. The mechanics of CFDs
3. Managing a CFD account
4. Trading strategies
5. Regulation
6. The future for CFDs

Introduction

The success rate for new financial trading products has traditionally been very low. However, occasionally a new product comes to light that fires the imagination and turns into a huge success. Take traded options for example. From their humble beginnings in an ante-room of the Chicago Board of Trade in the early 1970s, options fast became the derivative instrument of choice for fund managers, speculators, hedgers and arbitrageurs, so that today the global options business is colossal.

More recently, successful new trading products in global financial markets have expanded to include instruments like exchange traded funds (ETFs), spread bets, binary options and covered warrants.

But few have the capacity to be as successful over the long term as the Contract for Difference (CFD).

CFDs are becoming more popular in established CFD trading markets like Europe and Australia, and could potentially flourish once they are introduced in the US, Japan and China. At its current rate of expansion, the global market for CFDs could rival the trading volume of the cash markets of the underlying instruments that they are based on.

The history of CFDs

CFDs originated in the late 1980s as a response to demands from institutional traders and hedge funds to short stocks without having to undergo the awkward and often costly process of borrowing stock first.

The credit for creating the first CFD contracts has been attributed to the derivatives team at Smith New Court, a market maker in listed securities on the London Stock Exchange (LSE).

Traditionally, the only market participants allowed to go short of stock (that is, to sell stock they didn't already own in order to take advantage of falling stock prices) were professional equity market makers. But seeing the advantages of short selling that the market makers were enjoying, their clients also wanted an easier and more cost effective way to short stock than to borrow it first and then to sell it.

Equity market makers in large investment institutions started to offer CFDs as over-the-counter (OTC) products to institutional traders who were then able to take advantage of the tax exempt status of the product and the ability to hedge their portfolios. They then developed a range of speculative, risk-management and market neutral trading strategies.

Over the ensuing years this combination of factors, along with an increase in global equity market volatility, encouraged the CFD market to grow rapidly.

Retail interest in CFDs

In the late 1990s, while institutional traders were continuing to enjoy the benefits of trading CFDs, the retail sector became more interested in the product following the entrance of a significant institution to the retail market: Gerard and National Intercommodities (GNI).

GNI provided retail stock traders with the opportunity to trade CFDs on LSE stocks through its innovative front-end electronic trading system, GNI Touch, via a home computer connected to the Internet. GNI's retail service created the basis for retail stock traders to trade directly onto the Stock Exchange Electronic Trading Service (SETS) central limit order book at the LSE through a process known as Direct Market Access (DMA). For example, if a retail trader sent an order to buy a stock CFD, GNI would sell the CFD to the trader and then buy the equivalent stock position from the marketplace as a full hedge.

With access via GNI Touch to real-time bid and offer prices in UK listed stocks on the LSE, and the ability to leverage trading positions, the retail sector quickly embraced CFD trading. A number of European and UK institutions joined the CFD marketplace as it became clear that the product had several attractive attributes.

Attractions of CFDs

The reason why CFDs have become popular is a combination of the following:

1. CFDs can provide valuable **tax benefits**. For example, in the UK they are exempt from government stamp duty of 0.5% levied on regular stock purchase transactions.

2. As a low margined product they offer **leverage** to the price movements of a broad range of underlying instruments.

3. They offer the opportunity to go **short** of the underlying instrument without the need to engage in stock borrowing or additional funding.

4. They enable traders to transact business in a large variety of **underlying instruments** and create the basis for a broad range of **trading strategies**.

These attributes combine to make CFDs a very popular trading tool. For example, the tax benefits and the opportunity for leverage provide the ideal package for speculative trading. Unlike regular stock trading, market participants are able to gear their positions in CFDs to take advantage of price volatility, but are not penalised with costs associated with stamp duty for trading in and out of positions.

The outlook for CFDs

Today, there are over twenty CFD providers in Europe offering OTC trading services, enabling hedge funds, large and small institutional traders, semi professional and retail customers to trade CFDs.

Because CFDs originated in the UK the CFD providers offering global trading facilities are mainly UK companies, such as IG, GNI, CMC Markets, MF Global and others. European CFD providers, like Saxo Bank, and Australian CFD Providers, like Macquarie Bank and Prudential, have made significant inroads into providing global CFD markets over the past few years however.

With the recent increase in market volatility, CFD trading volume has increased. It is estimated that OTC CFD trading volume in the FTSE 100 index of UK listed stocks accounts for over 30% of total LSE SETS liquidity. This proportion of trading volume could grow over the coming years, not just on the LSE but on other exchanges, as traders start to recognise the benefits of trading CFDs in liquid listed products.

In addition, the CFD industry has grown significantly over the past two years as a result of the improved trading technology and functionality of CFD provider's trading systems. This technology has become much more user friendly and sophisticated. For example, some CFD provider's technology now enables traders to build their own automated trading strategies and to back test them on historical data before deploying them in live markets.

At the same time, most CFD providers have broadened the number of underlying instruments that customers are able to trade and also reduced the costs of trading. This has given rise to an increasing number of professional and semi professional traders who trade CFDs for a living.

In a recent development, The Australian Securities Exchange (ASX) introduced exchange-traded CFD contracts on a separate marketplace to its stock market in late 2007, adding to the product range available to traders in Australia as well as internationally. The benefit of a centrally-regulated product, with the added incentive of a centrally-managed clearing system via the central clearing counterparty (CCP), the SFE Clearing Corporation, is attractive to many traders. Through the *novation* process, whereby the clearing house stands between the buyer and the seller of the CFD contract, guaranteeing each at the point of registration of the contract, the SFE Clearing Corp effectively guarantees counterparty performance to other participating members.

Other exchanges around the world are also looking into the opportunity of listing CFD contracts of their own. Their technical infrastructure – with the predominant use of a central limit order book – creates the basis for high levels of liquidity which is conducive to new products like CFDs being introduced.

With greater access to global markets, a growing diversity and range of tradable instruments and a wider coverage of listed and OTC CFD products, the trading strategies that market participants use, are also becoming more sophisticated. The demand is now strong for cross asset CFD strategies and those that combine other derivatives, like options with CFDs

The future looks bright for the CFD product as can be seen from recent increases in trading volume and the increased product awareness across the different types of market participant.

1

The Principles of CFDs

What is a CFD?

Simply stated, a CFD is an informal contract between a broker (CFD provider) and his client where the client swaps the ownership of the physical stock for a contract with the broker that gives him the same economic interest.

A CFD is a contract then, not a tradable instrument. It is an agreement between a buyer and a CFD provider (who acts as the counterparty seller) to exchange the difference between the purchase price of the CFD and the price at which it is sold. The buyer of a CFD will profit if the underlying instrument on which the CFD is based rises in price and a seller will profit if the price falls.

Buying or selling a CFD is a proxy for buying or selling the underlying instrument. For the buyer, the benefits of a price rise in the underlying instrument will be passed on directly by the CFD provider.

Technical definition

For a more technical description of CFDs, try the following–

A CFD is a contract, or agreement, instigated on margin between a client and a CFD provider, to exchange the cash difference between the opening price and the closing price of a transaction in a given commodity upon the closing out of the open position.

So, a CFD is a primary derivative based on an underlying cash instrument, offering a flexible alternative to trading the underlying instrument by providing point-for-point price movement in line with the price movement of the cash instrument.

Equity CFDs

The best way to explain a stock CFD is to compare it to a traditional stock purchase through a broker.

- If a trader purchases **physical stock** through a broker the broker will process the order by trading with the exchange's electronic order book to buy physical stock on the trader's behalf. The stock purchase is then allocated to the trader's account. The broker charges his commission for transacting the deal, stamp duty is levied by the government of 0.5% of the value of the transaction, and the total value consideration of the trade is paid by the trader within three days, known as T+3, the settlement period laid down by the London Stock Exchange (the trading day plus 3 business days).

- If a trader buys a stock **CFD** through a broker, he must first lodge margin collateral with the broker in the form of cash or other accepted collateral form. The broker then writes the trader a contract for the entire order while simultaneously buying the stock on the exchange as a full hedge. The CFD broker then holds the stock, while the trader has a contract with the broker. The CFD trader does not trade directly with the exchange but deals with the broker as a third party. The trader then pays the broker commission, but as he has not physically bought stock, the trade is not subject to stamp duty. The contract with the broker is perpetual and does not have to be settled like the stock purchase after three days. If the stock price rises, the broker passes on the gains to the CFD trader's margin account; if the stock price falls, the broker requests additional funds from the trader to top up the margin account.

The thing to remember is that a CFD is a contract with a third party, not something tradable like a stock or a commodity; when a trader decides to sell the CFD he sells it back to the broker he bought it from.

Comparison with underlying instrument

There are important differences between trading an underlying security (e.g. a stock) and a CFD:

- Unlike an underlying instrument, such as a stock, the CFD is traded on **margin**. An amount of collateral is lodged with the CFD provider which enables the trader to purchase or sell a number of CFDs according to margin calculations that reflect an increased leverage over the stock purchase itself.

- The trader of a CFD contract **does not own the underlying instrument** but enters into an agreement with the CFD provider to exchange the cash difference in price between the opening price of the transaction and the closing price.

- A CFD can be traded **short** as well as long. The trader does not need to deliver the underlying security if he sells short.

- Currently, CFD trading does not attract UK government **stamp duty** of 0.5% but does qualify for capital gains tax on profits.

A CFD can be compared to:

- An **equity swap** with no expiration date that is financed by cash margin. The CFD is a derivative of the underlying and effectively swaps the benefits of trading the underlying instrument for a cash-margined product with greater leverage.

- A **single stock future**. As a leveraged product traded on margin, stock futures have similar characteristics to CFDs, except that they can be exercised into the underlying security, whereas CFDs on the whole cannot. There have been occasions when institutional customers have entered into agreements with the CFD-issuing provider to exchange the CFD for the underlying instrument, but this is not normal practice for most customers.

The following includes two simple examples of CFD trades: a long CFD trade and a short CFD trade.

1. Long CFD trade

A long CFD trade involves buying a CFD contract with the expectation that the price of the underlying stock is likely to rise.

Assumptions

- I expect the BP share price to **rise** from its current mid-price of £5.37.

- I have **£10,000 to place on margin.** My CFD provider offers me a maximum of 10 times my capital to trade with; so I could trade a position with a notional value of up to £100,000.

Trade

- I use a portion of my available trading capital to buy 10,000 CFDs from my CFD provider at the offer price of £5.38 per CFD. This gives me a position with a notional value of £53,800.

- Each day that I decide to hold my open long position, I *pay* a financing cost on the notional value of the position (£53,800) to the CFD provider. The interest rate used is 2% above the London Interbank Offered Rate (LIBOR) – which is currently at 4.5%.

- 10 days later, the BP share price has risen and I sell my 10,000 CFDs at £5.50.

The trade details are summarised in the following table.

	CFD position (£)
Margin available at 10X equity	100,000
Notional transaction value	53,800
Commission charged at 0.2%	(107.60)
Stamp duty (0.5%)	–
10 Days later the share price is at £5.50	
Financing charge at 2% above LIBOR for 10 days	6.50% x 10 x 53,800/360 = (97.14)
Notional transaction value	55,000
Commission charged at 0.2%	(110.00)
Profit minus costs	1200 – 314.74
Total profit	885.26

2. Short CFD trade

A short CFD trade involves selling a CFD contract with the expectation that the price of the underlying is likely to fall.

Assumptions

- I expect the BP share price to **fall** from its current mid-price of £5.37.

- I have **£10,000 to place on margin**. My CFD provider gives me 10 times my capital to trade with.

Trade

- I use a portion of my available capital to sell 10,000 CFDs to my CFD provider at the bid price of £5.36.

- Each day that I decide to hold my open short position, I *receive* a financing credit on the notional value of the position (£53,600). The interest rate used is 2% below the London Interbank Bid Rate (LIBID) – which is currently at 3.75%.

- 10 days later, the BP share price has fallen and I buy back 10,000 CFDs at £5.25.

The trade details are summarised in the following table.

	CFD position (£)
Margin available at 10x equity	100,000
Notional transaction value	53,600
Commission charged at 0.2%	(107.20)
Stamp duty (0.5%)	–
10 days later the share price is at £5.25	
Financing credit at 2% below LIBID for 10 days	1.75% x 10 x 53,600/360 = 26.06
Notional transaction value	52,500
Commission charged at 0.2%	(105.00)
Profit minus costs	1100 – 186.14
Total profit	913.86

Range of CFDs

The range of CFDs that a trader is able to trade depends on his CFD provider and which underlying instruments they are willing to issue CFDs on. A CFD provider normally offers a range of instruments to choose from including global stocks, bonds, commodities, and currency pairs, as well as a range of stock or commodity indices and sector indices.

CFDs appeal to traders because of the broad range of products that are available, especially as traders have the added advantage of being able to trade CFDs in non-domestically traded instruments – so that a UK or European trader can trade CFDs in US stocks.

The range of global markets and instruments that are covered is now extensive, and new opportunities for access to CFDs on different markets are continuously available. The main categories of instrument include:

- global equity CFDs (e.g. UK, US, Asian and European)

- government bond CFDs

- sector CFDs (e.g. oil and gas, banks, technology)

- stock index CFDs (e.g. FTSE, Dow, NASDAQ, NIKKEI)

- FX CFDs

- commodity CFDs (e.g. softs, grains)

- metals and energy CFDs (e.g. gold, silver, oil, natural gas)

In principle, CFDs could exist on almost any traded instrument in the world. In practice, a trader's access to CFDs is only limited by what his CFD provider is willing to offer him.

The table below shows an estimated breakdown of trading activity in CFDs and FX. The information was collated from three CFD providers.

CFD product	Estimated trading activity average (100%)
European stocks	10%
UK stocks	15%
US stocks	15%
Stock index	15%
FX (non-CFD)	30%
Bond	5%
Commodities	10%

As can be seen in the preceding table FX trading was the highest percentage trading activity with the three providers. FX trades in Europe are predominantly outside of the CFD product arena but FX CFDs do exist. The Australian Stock Exchange (ASX) offers FX CFDs on many currency pairs.

What types of CFD are there?

CFDs are offered in unlisted, listed and exchange traded form.

Unlisted CFDs

The majority of CFD products are currently in unlisted form: they are over-the-counter in nature (i.e. they aren't traded on an exchange) and take the form of a contract between the trader and their CFD provider.

This means that CFD positions can only be closed out with the counterparty (the provider) that issued them.

Financing costs are deducted from holders of open long CFD positions or paid to sellers of open short CFD positions on a daily basis. Trading commissions are also deducted when CFD trades are opened and closed, additional margin payments may also be due at the discretion of the provider if the open position moves into a loss.

Listed CFDs

Listed CFDs are available in several European countries, but for this example I will take the UK Listed CFD market.

UK Listed CFDs (also referred to as *Turbos*) are approved for trading by the Financial Services Authority (FSA) with trading taking place on the LSE. Listed CFDs are generic to the UK market and are provided by a single issuer, Société Générale.

Listed CFD issuers are obliged to maintain a dealing bid-offer spread throughout the trading day from 8.15am to 4.30pm so that there is always a ready market for trades. This two-way dealing spread is made publically available on the LSE (unlike CFD bid and offer prices from OTC CFD providers).

With listed CFDs, all financing costs and commissions and dividends are incorporated in the trading price so there are no additional charges to fund. Instead, the CFD price is adjusted daily for daily financing costs. Listed CFDs also have other notable characteristics:

- They have an embedded guaranteed stop loss meaning that the CFD trader cannot lose more than the initial margin payment they pay.

- There are no additional margin calls. The CFD position remains open until the trader closes it or the stop loss level has been met.

- They have an expiry date unlike OTC CFDs.

- Because trading and pricing is undertaken on the LSE there is better counterparty protection against a default compared with an unlisted CFD traded with an OTC provider which is a direct contract with a third party financial institution.

- As stock exchange listed contracts they can be traded through registered UK stockbrokers but not directly with SG.

- Commissions are paid on the initial margin payment, not the full trade value of the open CFD position.

- All listed CFDs are subject to Capital Gains Tax and are eligible as constituents of SIPP accounts but not of ISAs.

Exchange-traded CFDs

Standardised CFD contracts

While traditionally CFDs have been OTC products whereby the CFD trader dealt with the CFD provider as the counterparty to the trade, now there is demand for more standardised contracts where an exchange issues the CFD on a regulated exchange marketplace and a central clearing counterparty (CCP) acts as buyer to every seller and seller to every buyer (as it currently does for stock and futures trading).

As mentioned previously, the Australian Securities Exchange (ASX) introduced exchange-traded CFDs (ASX CFDs) on a separate electronic market to the cash market in late 2007. They look similar to unlisted CFDs but have the following advantages:

1. they are cleared by the Australian central clearing house (CCP), the SFE Clearing Corporation, that stands as a guarantor between every buyer and seller,

2. the contracts are based on standardised contract definitions, and

3. the exchange upholds the credibility, transparency and security of the marketplace.

The ASX's objective is to increase the competition between market makers (of which there are at least six) who provide competitive bids and offers. This competition is expected to reduce the size of the bid-offer spread.

With the use of a CCP, the margin required from CFD traders with open positions is likely to be lower than in the over-the-counter market. There is also full anonymity with regard to open CFD positions transacted on the ASX.

Which countries can you trade CFDs in?

CFD trading is well established in the UK, Australia, parts of central Europe, South Africa and Singapore, and is spreading to other areas of the globe including other countries in Europe, China, Korea and Japan.

To give an example of the phenomenal rate of growth in CFD trading in Europe, the forecast is for the number of CFD traders in Germany to increase by a factor of six times over the next 3-5 years. This means the number of traders in CFDs would rise from its current level of 40,000 to a number nearer 250,000 in this period.

Broadly speaking, similar benefits of trading CFDs exist in each country but there are subtle differences in the handling of factors such as tax and CFD margin issues. For example, the Monetary Authority of Singapore (MAS) sets the minimum margin rates for trading CFDs rather than letting independent CFD providers set their own levels. And while the UK government favours an unregulated product (a spreadbet) by exempting spreadbetting profits from capital gains tax, it does not exempt profits from trading a regulated product, a CFD. Germany, on the other hand, treats spreadbets and CFDs in the same way with regard to taxable profits, both being subject to capital gains tax.

Although the trading benefits of CFDs for traders in many countries are clear, financial market regulators of certain countries will not permit their citizens to trade in them. For example, while the UK, Germany, Switzerland, Italy, Spain, Singapore, South Africa, Australia and New Zealand currently allow trading in CFDs, the US and Canada do not.

Types of CFD provider

There are two main types of CFD provider:

1. broker (or agent or intermediary), and

2. market maker.

Some providers combine both functions. These two types are explained in more detail below.

1. CFD broker

CFD providers who act as *brokers* (also called *agents* or *intermediaries*) charge a commission for providing a CFD trading service. They assume a riskless position based upon the order flow generated by the customer by automatically generating an equivalent transaction of the customer's CFD order in the underlying market to hedge their contract with the customer.

Example

For example, if a customer sends an order to buy 100 Volkswagen CFDs, the broker will buy 100 Volkswagen shares on the German stock market XETRA and sell 100 CFDs to the customer. In this way, the broker is providing the customer with an equivalent position in the stock, while maintaining a riskless position – with each movement of the underlying instrument being reflected in the price movement of the CFD. The broker will hold the open stock position in Volkswagen until the customer decides to sell his CFDs. Then the reverse transaction takes place. The customer sends an order to the broker to sell 100 CFDs, the broker sells 100 Volkswagen shares on XETRA and simultaneously buys 100 CFDs from the customer to close the position.

The broker will charge a commission for having traded with the customer and will charge a financing fee for having to hold 100 shares of Volkswagen on the client's behalf.

Note: In some cases the product terms define 1 CFD contract as equal to 100 shares. It is completely flexible, with the terms decided by the CFD provider. However, in most cases 1 CFD covers 1 share – and that ratio will be assumed in the rest of this book (unless otherwise specified).

So, an agent CFD provider is still counterparty to a customer CFD order, but immediately hedges the transaction in the underlying instrument on the exchange, thus mitigating risk and providing the customer with any price improvements upon execution.

CFD broker order flow

The following diagram shows the flow of order activity when a CFD trader buys a CFD from a broker. The CFD trader is looking to take an economic interest in 10,000 shares and sends an order to the CFD broker to buy 10,000 CFDs, while paying a margin of 10% of the notional value of the position. The CFD broker writes a CFD for the amount of shares requested and simultaneously buys 10,000 shares from the market to cover his risk.

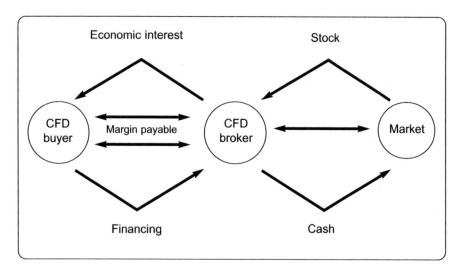

2. CFD market maker

Unlike the CFD broker *agent* who passes through the customer's CFD order to the marketplace with a trade in the underlying instrument, a CFD *market maker* can assume the risk of the trade by taking on proprietary positions as a result of customer order flow. The CFD market maker also provides bespoke price quotes for customers to transact with, creating a bid-offer spread outside of the underlying market environment.

The CFD market maker is at liberty to assume the risk of the customer CFD order and makes a price quotation based upon the underlying instrument, but is not obliged to hedge that transaction in the market. CFD market makers quote prices in CFDs based upon the price of the underlying security but with bid-offer spreads that reflect their own trading position and opinion of the market. The width of the bid-offer spread is dictated by the market maker's own proprietary book position and the best execution requirements of the European regulatory directive, MiFID. Depending on the liquidity and volatility of the underlying instrument, market makers may offer narrower or wider dealing spreads.

CFD providers who are brokers earn commissions on CFD transactions whereas CFD market makers profit from the dealing bid-offer spread they impose.

CFD market maker order flow

The following diagram shows the flow of order activity when a CFD trader buys a CFD from a market maker. The CFD trader is looking to take an economic interest in 10,000 BP shares and sends an order to the CFD market maker to buy 10,000 CFDs, while paying margin of 10% on the notional value of the position. The CFD market maker writes a CFD for the amount of shares requested and then has a choice of offsetting the risk of the position with his internal order book, or hedging by buying 10,000 shares from the market to cover his risk.

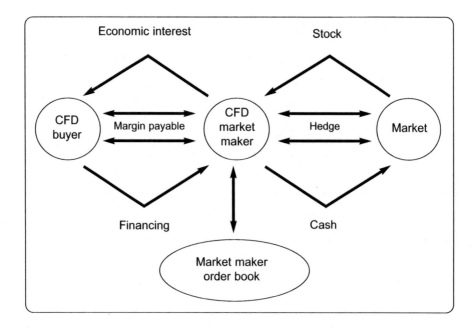

Market makers are skilled in judging the price movements of the instruments they trade. Their profitability arises from their ability to manage a portfolio of open positions generated in the most part by their customer order flow and their interpretation of market activity.

How CFDs are traded

It is useful at this stage to describe briefly the evolution of electronic traded markets in order to show how the creation of an electronic central limit order book paved the way for the increased growth in equity CFD trading.

I use the London Stock Exchange as an example here but the same efficiencies that electronic trading provides with direct market access, pricing efficiency and liquidity apply equally to other global markets. For most active CFD traders, participation in the live limit order book of an exchange is a crucial component to their trading. Without access to the immediacy of the exchange's own order book they would be reliant on second-hand information with regard to prices and quotes, and would not be able to see the depth of market with regard to the bids and offers being placed at prices outside of the best bid-offer quotation.

It is clear that without the creation and development of an electronic central limit order book – that is accessible to traders through a range of financial intermediaries – the CFD market would not be as big as it is today.

Development of electronic trading platforms

SEAQ

With the advent of electronic trading in London in 1986, following the City's Big Bang, the London Stock Exchange introduced the SEAQ (Stock Exchange Automated Quotation) market making system. The objective was to provide a central forum for market maker quotations in London stocks and to provide bid-offer spreads that were transparent in a minimum number of shares.

The SEAQ platform was quote-driven and relied upon orders being executed via the telephone with one of the two or more market makers associated with each stock, rather than through the electronic click functionality of a trading computer.

However, SEAQ had its limitations. Although less liquid stocks benefited from the quote-driven style of platform, stocks that were more liquid required a more immediate transaction capability, and it became obvious that they would benefit from participating in an order-driven quotation environment.

SETS

As a result, in 1997, the LSE introduced SETS (Stock Exchange Electronic Trading Service) to provide an electronic, order-driven, central limit order book in the top companies quoted on the LSE.

SETS revolutionised the trading activity on the LSE, paving the way for the use of electronically generated order flow through automated trading systems and the prolific use of order management techniques like Volume Weighted Average Price (VWAP), Time Weighted Average Price (TWAP), and performance measurement assessment through Transaction Cost Analysis (TCA).

The playing field is levelled for small traders and large institutions

The introduction of SETS also spurred the liberation of the non-professional and semi-professional trader from the direct management of their trades by broker intermediaries, enabling them to enter orders directly via electronic trading systems that were autonomous of intermediary interference.

This disintermediation of the financial markets is continuing, with many active individual traders assuming a similar status as small institutions of a few years back.

SETS also provided a fertile ground for new trading opportunities with the introduction of an opening and closing auction and continuous trading for eight and a half hours each business day.

Live limit order book access to SETS is referred to as Level II access, and it provides a breakdown of all the bids and offers sent in electronically from all customers of the exchange.

The benefit of using SETS is that it provides an efficient, transparent and cost-effective means of trading, matching the best bids and offers of buyers and sellers using a price/time priority matching algorithm. That is, orders that are sent to the exchange matching engine are ranked first according to their price and then the time at which they reached the order book. In this way, depending on their form of electronic access, retail and semi-professional traders have as much chance to place their orders higher in the order queue as other market participants, including professional traders and market makers.

In effect, the centralisation of order flow on SETS results in narrower dealing spreads and cheaper exchange fees.

London Stock Exchange SETS order book

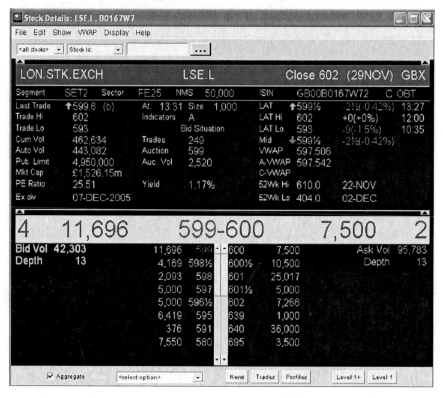

The SETS order book in the example shows the following:

- The **upper section** of the screen has a number of statistics including last trade price, traded highs and lows, the cumulative daily volume, VWAP price and change of price on the day, among others.

- The **lower band** running horizontally across the screen shows the best bid and offer in the stock and the bid and ask volumes. In this case, the best (highest) bid is 599 for 11,696 shares, the best (lowest) offer is 600 for 7500 shares.

- The **lower section** lists the other bids and offers in the market at those prices below the best bid and above the best offer.

CFDs and direct market access (DMA)

As a result of the demand for access to the SETS order book, most UK CFD providers now provide direct access for their customers to SETS by way of an electronic network connection known as Direct Market Access (DMA).

DMA enables CFD traders to effectively trade directly within the limit order book of the underlying marketplace. For example, when a customer submits a CFD order to an agent provider, the provider takes a position on behalf of the customer in the underlying market, which the customer can see via the SETS trading screen. Although the customer is trading the CFD, the open position the CFD provider has taken in the underlying instrument replicates the customer's CFD order. In this way, the customer is deemed to be participating directly in the trading behaviour of the underlying instrument in the live market, as the CFD price action moves in unison with the price activity of the underlying instrument.

DMA is a popular market access process because of the transparency it provides, and the opportunity that CFD traders have to enter market and limit orders that fall within the best bid-offer spreads of the underlying instrument. Customer's OTC CFD orders are therefore fully reflected in the central limit order book on the exchange host's trading platform.

Arguably, by using DMA to submit orders into SETS, CFD traders are able to participate in larger pools of liquidity than if they were trading with a single CFD market maker as counterparty.

Access to the central limit order book of LSE SETS is now a prerequisite for UK equity CFD traders, as CFD limit bids and offers are represented in the limit order book through the associated stock order entered by the CFD agent. This is a great step forward for traders of all levels of expertise, as direct access to live central limit order books was not traditionally available to them even just a few years ago.

DMA to European equity markets is also popular, in particular the German stock market XETRA and Euronext with their broad range of large cap European companies and equity indices.

Characteristics of CFDs

In this section we will look at some specific characteristics of CFDs such as the relationship between a CFD and its underlying instrument, the practice of leverage, dealing spreads and counterparty risks.

As mentioned earlier in the book, there are some fundamental qualities that CFDs have that make them different to other instruments: not having an expiry date, the benefits of leverage, favourable tax treatment in the UK and the ability to go short of a stock without borrowing it first.

However, it is important to remember that the profitability of an open position can be influenced by elements other than the price movement of the underlying instrument. Traders should not underestimate the impact of financing costs on open positions as these are additional to margin requirements.

The relationship of a CFD to its underlying

CFD prices reflect the real-time bid-offer price of the underlying instruments, be they a listed security, commodity or a currency pair.

The quoted price of a CFD moves in direct correlation to the price movement of the underlying security, normally point for point because the CFD replicates the per point movement of the underlying. The market price of the underlying is quoted directly to the CFD trader without amendment so that the CFD bid and offer is the same as that of the underlying. If the trader sends an order based on the underlying dealing spread, the CFD provider, unless they are a market maker, matches the order at the price given in the underlying market by writing a contract. The CFD provider will simultaneously trade in the underlying market to hedge the written contract, looking only to take a commission from the deal. An example will illustrate this in more detail.

Example

Barclays Bank share has a bid-offer quote of 336p-336.5p on SETS at the LSE. The CFD provider is also showing a bid-offer quote of 336p-336.5p. If the trader wants to buy 10,000 CFDs, he will pay the offer price of 336.5p as long as the quoted volume at this price enables him to do so.

When the CFD order is placed, the CFD provider buys the 10,000 shares (at 336.5p) and sells to the trader 10,000 CFDs. Until the trader closes the CFD open long position, the CFD provider will keep the 10,000 shares, selling them to close when the trader sells his CFDs. Throughout the period during which the trader has kept his open position, the 10,000 CFDs contract behaves like 10,000 shares except that the trader does not own the shares. The CFD price will move exactly in line with the underlying share price so that when the trader decides to close out his position, he will sell at the prevailing bid price in the market as long as the volume is present at that price.

There should be no divergence in the share price correlation between the CFD and the underlying share during the life of the transaction. The difference in the performance of the share and the CFD with regard to profit or loss depends on the degree of leverage the open CFD position has and this will be explained below.

Dealing spreads

CFD dealing spreads refer to the gap between the bid price and the offer price. If you decide to sell short, you will hit the bid price (which is the lower of the two quoted prices), and if you decide to buy and go long you will take the offer price (which is the higher of the two).

The spread, which in the case of actively traded stocks like Vodafone, can be as little as a tenth of a penny, represents a cost, above the commissions, that the trade must recover before it goes into profit.

The following example will demonstrate this.

	CFD bid price (pence)	CFD offer price (pence)
Dealing spread = 0.5	200.00	200.50
Sell 10,000 CFDs at bid price	Sell at 200.00	
Buy 10,000 CFDs at offer price		Buy at 200.50
Notional value	£20,000	£20,050

As can be seen from the example, ignoring commissions, the dealing spread has cost the CFD trader £50 because the price must move at least by 0.5p in the right direction for him to see a profit.

Traders need to be careful to factor into their profit and loss expectations the width of bid-offer spreads that CFD providers quote.

Agency brokers

Agency CFD providers are expected to replicate the spread behaviour of the underlying traded instrument. As such, the size of the CFD bid-offer spread is dependent on the bid-offer spread in the underlying. For example, when placing a limit order in an LSE-listed stock through a CFD provider who is a broker, CFD traders participate directly in the exchange's central limit order book (SETS). The CFD order is automatically placed into the limit order book as a corresponding stock order. If the CFD order is in a commodity, then the prevailing bid-offer spread in the underlying instrument will also determine the price of the CFD.

Market makers

A CFD market maker, who makes his own prices, may widen bid-offer spreads during times of market volatility or withdraw tradable prices altogether given unfavourable market conditions.

For example, in the run-up to a sensitive economic announcement, like the publication of US Non-Farm Payrolls, or a company results announcement, the CFD market maker may cease quoting prices if the risk associated with becoming excessively long or short as a result of customer orders becomes too great.

Like other investments, the size of the bid-offer spread on a CFD will determine how quickly an open position is likely to become profitable. The wider the bid-offer spread the more the price of an underlying asset must move in order to make a trade profitable.

The dealing spread that some CFD providers – particularly CFD market makers – charge varies enormously depending on the width of the dealing spread in the underlying market. The table below gives examples of the CFD provider's spread in addition to the dealing spread in the underlying market.

CFD	Dealing spread over the market spread
Coffee	0.8
London No.7 Cocoa	6.0
Gasoil	200
Australian 10 Year Bond	0.03

Leverage

The opportunity to trade on margin and therefore to utilise leverage has revolutionised the financial services industry in recent years. Current levels of leveraged trading are high due to the growing popularity of spread betting and CFD trading as an alternative to cash instrument trading. Leveraging enables the CFD trader to gear a long or short position in a selected underlying so that each incremental increase or decrease in the share price has an exaggerated effect on the profitability or loss of an open CFD position.

An example of the gearing effect on profitability through leverage can be seen in the table below, which compares two positions, one long 10,000 shares, the other long 100,000 CFDs. The margin paid by the CFD trader is 10% and both the share buyer and the CFD trader have £50,000 at their disposal. The share price incremental movements increase by 1p, 5p, 10p, 20p, and 30p and commissions are excluded.

Share price movement	Long share profit (£)	Long CFD profit (£)
+1p	100	1000
+5p	500	5000
+10p	1000	10,000
+20p	2000	20,000
+30p	3000	30,000

As can be seen from the table, the CFD trader's profitability outstrips the share buyer by a considerable amount. This is because the CFD trader is able to secure an open position of 100,000 CFDs as opposed to 10,000 (due to the 10% margin) and has higher gearing as a result.

What are the risks of using leverage to trade CFDs?

Trading CFDs has its risks as well as benefits. Leverage can work positively and negatively, so a trader may be asked to provide additional margin if the position starts to go into loss. Profits and losses respond to leverage at some 10 times (if the margin is 10%) the rate of the change in the price of the underlying instruments because of gearing.

The leverage that is created by CFDs means that the trader is able to take advantage of very small changes in the price movement of the traded instrument. If the underlying instrument price move causes the CFD to go into profit, the CFD trader can enjoy the benefits of the highly leveraged position, but heightened risk enters the equation if the price of the traded instrument moves abruptly into loss. Because of the gearing associated with the transaction, any losses are magnified in the same manner that profits are magnified.

Leverage is a wonderful thing when the market is moving in an anticipated direction, but when things turn sour the potential loss is also amplified.

Tick values

Tick values represent the value of a single currency unit movement up or down of the price of a traded CFD product. So if a trader buys or sells a single CFD in gold that has a tick value of 1 and the price moves from 875 to 876 then the value of the increase is $1. Tick movements vary considerably between products.

The following table gives some examples:

Product	Tick value (US$)
Copper CFD	0.05
Gold CFD	1.00
GBP/USD currency CFD	0.0001
US S&P 500 index CFD	1.00
EURO/JPY currency CFD	0.01
Live cattle CFD	0.025

The base currency of accounts

When you trade CFDs, you are always trading in the base currency of the underlying cash instrument or market. For example, if you trade a European share CFD, you will be trading in euros, while a US share CFD will trade in US dollars.

Your trading account with the CFD provider is denominated in one 'reporting' currency, so that if the CFD provider's designated reporting currency is US dollars for all CFD trading accounts, all CFD transactions with various currency denominations will form a ledger balance that is converted to the reporting currency on a daily basis or at a regular interval chosen by you. The conversion normally takes place at 22.00 hours.

Sub-accounts are designated by CFD providers for each currency that the CFD trader is trading in. For example, traders who wish to trade in US dollar, euro and GBP denominated CFDs will have three sub-accounts. Traders are able to fund these sub-accounts in the designated currency and can maintain their currency levels without having to convert to the reporting currency of the main account every day.

In order to convert all CFD transactions denominated in different currencies, a foreign exchange transaction, or conversion, is enacted at the prevailing exchange rate plus a percentage (sometimes up to 0.5%) of the currency consideration by the CFD Provider.

Do CFDs expire?

CFDs based on cash equities do not have fixed expiry dates; whereas commodity, treasury and index CFDs normally do have fixed expiry dates which are based on the expiry dates of the underlying futures contract on which the CFD contract is based.

For example, some CFD providers will set an expiry date for US Treasury 10 Year notes for the last business day of the month previous to the futures expiry month, so if the futures contract expires in March, the CFD will expire on the last business day of February.

Expiry dates vary for commodity instruments depending on the rules set by the CFD provider and the futures expiry for the commodity. For example, coffee CFDs can expire on the last business day of the month previous to the futures expiry, whereas corn CFDs can expire on the third Friday of the previous month to the futures expiry. US crude oil CFDs can expire the trading day immediately before the underlying futures contract expiry.

CFD rollover near to expiration

If an open CFD position is getting close to expiry it may be closed out automatically by the CFD provider if it is not closed or rolled over by the trader. However, CFD traders can avoid automatic close-out by rolling the open position into a new far contract with a longer-dated expiry. This rollover facility is available normally a month before the near month CFD contract is due to expire giving the CFD trader plenty of time to roll the open position into the next expiry period if he so wishes.

The mechanics behind the rollover process require the closing out of the existing near expiry position at the mid-price of the CFD bid-offer spread and the opening of an equal position in the new far month contract. By rolling over the position, the CFD trader may incur a loss or a profit which will immediately be visible in the trader's trading account. Some CFD providers reduce the rollover cost to the trader by allowing the trade to be rolled over at half of the bid-offer spread rate.

Trading hours

CFD providers offer trading services normally within the opening hours of the chosen exchange or marketplace. If a CFD trader decides to trade a German stock CFD, for example, then he must buy or sell that stock CFD within the opening hours of the German stock exchange, unless the CFD provider offers an opportunity to trade out of hours.

Traded markets are normally designated as "24 hours" or "Exchange Hours" markets. Twenty-four-hour markets like forex (FX), for example, trade continuously unless there is a technical interruption in the marketplace or the CFD provider's network closes it for a short period. CFD providers normally state their opening times in their business terms and conditions, with some sticking to exchange hours while others open more frequently. For example, some CFD providers will offer an open late on Sunday evenings at 20.00 hours and close on Friday nights at 22.00 hours.

It is advisable to know the exact trading timetable of the CFD provider for each market being traded in to avoid being late to close an open position.

It is also worth noting that CFD dealing spreads can widen when the market approaches exchange opening and closing times and out of exchange hours if markets become more volatile.

Counterparty risk

Dealing with a UK stockbroker when buying shares on a regulated European exchange, like the LSE for example, means that the trader is protected by the regulatory institution that oversees the stockbroker and the exchange, in this case the FSA. In addition, the exchanges have central clearing counterparties (CCPs) who act as the seller to every buyer and the buyer to every seller so as to eliminate counterparty risk on the trading platform.

However, the risks of dealing directly with a CFD provider are different. If a trader buys a CFD from a CFD provider he is dealing in a principle-to-principle transaction rather than an agency-to-principle transaction (as he would do in a transaction with, say, a stockbroker); the deal he is striking is with the CFD provider, not the CCP. This means that the same guarantees are not present for the CFD trader as the share trader through his broker. In effect, the CFD trader has counterparty risk with the CFD provider.

Counterparty risks include safety of deposited funds, the potential insolvency of the CFD provider, potential problems when it comes to disputes to do with transactions and general accountability. There are simple checks that can be made by the CFD trader before he signs up to a new provider. For example, the CFD provider should state that client's deposited funds should be kept in a separate customer funds account and not used in conjunction with general operating expenses. In addition, the CFD trader should find out if client's funds are protected by an underwriter in the form of a certificate of insurance (under the headings, 'General Commercial' and 'Endorsement: Client account segregation'). Always check the dates of the certificate as, occasionally, the documents presented are out of date.

In addition, it would be advisable to note if the CFD provider has a fidelity bond and whether it covers the funds of clients of the company as well as the company itself. A fidelity bond is a form of protection designed to cover policy holders against the fraudulent activities of an employee.

The CFD trader should read the CFD Provider's 'Memorandum of Articles and Associations' to ascertain their corporate status, their share capital and their categories of business, and the 'Terms of Business' document to find out more about the way in which the provider expects to deal with risks to customers and their money.

Comparison of CFDs with other instruments

CFDs share some characteristics with other derivatives, such as futures, covered warrants, options and spread bets. The following table compares the main characteristics of these instruments.

	CFD	Futures	Covered warrant	Options	Spread bets
Margin required	1–20%	5–10%	N/A	5–10%	1–20%
Dividend adjustment	Yes, 90% receivable for longs, 100% payable for shorts	Yes	No	Yes	No
Commission	0.1–0.25% of total transaction consideration, or dealing spread only	£1.50–4.00 per transaction	0.2–0.5%	£1.50–4.00 per transaction	No
Spreads	Deal at cash market price or with market maker spread	Tight in index futures; less tight in stock futures	0.5–1 bp	Tight in index options and liquid stock options	Varies with product and firm. Less on daily positions
Product specifics	Non-callable derivative	Non-callable derivative	Callable derivative with strike price	Callable derivative with strike price	Non-callable derivative
Pricing	Same as cash underlying	Futures fair value based on carry model	Long dated options pricing model	Options pricing model	Defined per point stake
Stock borrowing requirement?	No	No	No	No	No
UK stamp duty	No	If stock futures exercised	If exercised into underlying stock	If exercised into underlying stock	No
CGT on gains	Yes	Yes	Yes	Yes	No

2

The Mechanics of CFDs

CFDs are not complex instruments. And they do share some similarities with other derivatives, differing only in detail. However, in the case of CFDs, it is the detail that is important. It is only by understanding the detail – for example, the seemingly innocuous financing charges – that the true nature of CFDs can be understood.

So, this chapter is about the detail!

This chapter describes the mechanics of CFDs, covering first the money flows of a trade and then looking at how corporate actions affect equity CFDs.

Money flows of a trade

This section will look closely at the money flows of a trade, including:

1. Margin

2. Commissions

3. Financing costs (including long-term funding of a CFD position and financing currency CFDs)

4. Tax

5. Detailed worked example

1. Margin

Margin is an amount of money paid upfront by a customer to a CFD provider to guarantee performance of the CFD contract. In effect, the margin paid is designed to protect the CFD provider to prevent a case where the customer incurs a loss on his position and can't pay.

Margin has been used for many years to provide traders with the opportunity to trade derivative instruments like futures and options. The same principle applies to CFD margining as it does to futures margining.

An initial deposit, referred to as initial margin (or the notional trading requirement, NTR in the CFD world) is required before a new position can be opened by a trader. Once a trader has opened a new trade, he must maintain the margin deposit above the level of anticipated losses when managing an open position. This is known as *variation margin*.

Initial margin

In most markets the level of initial margin will be set independently by each CFD provider. When they come to decide on the level of the margin rate they will take into account the volatility of the underlying instrument. In this exercise the CFD provider is trying to forecast the loss that a position may suffer during one trading session (or over whatever the shortest period is between margin calls). The intention is for any loss on a client's position during a trading session to be covered by the client's funds that the CFD provider *already* holds (in the form of margin).

The usual way to estimate the likely loss for an instrument during a trading session is to look at its trading patterns in the past (i.e. to calculate its *historic volatility*). For example, if an instrument has fluctuated within a band of approximately 1% in past trading sessions, then the margin rate will be set around this figure.

Historic volatility

Margin levels vary depending on the type of instrument that the CFD trader is buying or selling. The more risky an instrument (i.e. the greater its volatility) then the higher the margin rate. For example, stock index CFDs may attract a margin rate of 5%, whereas an individual stock CFD may have a margin rate of 10% – because individual stocks are usually more volatile than stock indices. Margin rates on forex CFDs can be just 2%.

Market volatility

While the historic volatility of the individual instrument is an important consideration for margin, so is the current volatility of the market as a whole. If the market is in a highly volatile state, this will make the provider more likely to increase margin rates for instruments traded in that market.

Notional value

Having set the margin rate, this will then be applied to *notional value* (i.e. the size of the trade). The notional value of a trade is the size of the exposure to the underlying asset. For example, a trade of 10,000 Vodafone CFDs (when the Vodafone share price is 116p) would have a notional value for the position of £11,600 (10,000 x £1.16).

Note: Margin rates are not carved in stone: the rates can vary over time as market conditions change, and rates also differ between CFD providers.

Variation margin

Variation Margin is calculated throughout the trading day by the CFD provider by comparing the price of the traded instrument when the CFD trade was opened and the current traded price. This comparison is known as *mark-to-market* and can be continuously calculated, periodically assessed or determined at the end of the trading day depending on the volatility of the instrument and the CFD provider's internal rules.

If the level of margin available in the trader's CFD account falls beneath the minimum required value due to an adverse movement in the CFD price, a margin call may be made by the CFD provider requesting additional funds to be deposited into the margin account (to cover the losses incurred on the position and to restore the required minimum margin level).

Margin groups

As all trading instruments behave in different ways, they are assessed for margin purposes and placed into margin groups, depending on the level of their perceived riskiness.

Stock CFDs, for example, are subject to margin requirements that are based upon their market capitalisation, liquidity and volatility. Below is an example of the minimum margin requirements of different stock CFDs. Whereas stock indices and lower-risk stocks attract a minimum margin requirement of around 5% and 10%, CFD traders can expect to have to put up 100% of the value of an underlying security if the minimum margin requirement is 100% and the traded instrument is deemed to be extremely risky.

Margin group	Category	Minimum margin required
Group 1	Indices and low risk stocks	5%
Group 2	Low-medium risk stocks	10%
Group 3	Medium risk stocks	15%
Group 4	High risk stocks	25%
Group 5	Very high risk stocks	50%
Group 6	Extreme risk stocks	100%

Source: Saxo Bank

For UK top 100 FTSE index equity CFDs for example, the margin at the time of writing is in the region of 5-10% for experienced traders, and up to 20% for less experienced traders. This means that with a margin level of 10%, an experienced trader can put down as little as £10,000 to open a position with a nominal value of £100,000. As volatility in the equity markets subsides or increases over time margin rates will also fall and rise.

An open CFD position will be marked to market each day. That is, the value of the open position will be calculated against the trade value of the traded instrument, and if additional margin is required, it will be calculated by way of its relationship to the notional trading requirement, NTR.

If a trader takes on a new open CFD position to the value of £50,000, for example, and the CFD provider has stated that the NTR is 10%, the customer will be required to deposit an NTR of £5000 (representing 10% of the value of the underlying position).

The NTR is calculated using the following equation:

Trade size x trade value x NTR percentage

So, for example, where a customer is trading 20 CFDs with a trade value of £750.00 and the NTR is 10%:

20 x £750.00 x 0.1 = £1500

If the customer does not maintain the correct NTR or the open position moves into loss, the CFD provider will issue a margin call asking the trader to deposit more money into his margin account.

Margin Q&A

The following details are based on information derived from Saxo Bank. Other CFD providers may slightly differ in respect to their finance and margin details, but broadly speaking, the following can be taken as representative.

1. If I transfer £15,000 in funds to a CFD provider and I then open a position that requires margin of £10,000, what happens to my remaining £5000? Do I receive interest on the net free equity?

Not necessarily. It all depends on the deposit value threshold above which the CFD provider is prepared to pay interest. Some CFD providers require more than £5000 net free equity in the main trading account before they will pay interest. Interest on the main account is calculated on the net free equity and interest on the sub-accounts is calculated on the account value.

However since the net free equity is calculated on open trade positions on all the CFD trader's accounts it is important to make sure that sufficient cash is available on the main account. Otherwise you risk being subject to a debit interest on your main account exceeding the credit interest payable on your sub-account(s).

Net free equity

Net free equity is a term used by many CFD providers and is defined as:

- the cash balance on the main trading account,

- plus or minus the value of any unrealised profits or losses from open trade exposures in CFDs, and other instruments that may make up the constituents of the main trading account

- minus the value of the CFD provider's margin requirements for open trade positions on all accounts.

Account value

Account value is defined as:

- the cash balance on the individual sub-account

- plus or minus the value of any unrealised profits or losses from open trade exposures in CFDs and other instruments that make up the constituents of the sub-account

Retail interest rates

Here is an example of the interest rates that can apply to funds deposited with a CFD provider:

- in this case the CFD provider does not pay interest on either the main account or the sub-account on sums up to USD 15,000 (or the currency equivalent);

- the CFD provider pays interest on positive net free equity and account value exceeding USD 15,000 up to USD 100,000, at LIBID minus 3% on the full amount;

- for positive net free equity and account value exceeding USD 100,000 – the CFD provider pays interest at LIBID minus 2% on the full amount;

- on the other hand, for negative net free equity and account value interest is charged at LIBOR plus 3%.

Institutional interest rates

The following interest rates apply to funds deposited by financial institutions with the CFD Provider:

- for positive net free equity interest will be paid at LIBID minus 1% on the full amount for all account values

- for negative net free equity interest will be charged at LIBOR plus 1% on the full amount for all account values

Calculation and settlement

With this CFD provider interest is calculated daily and settled monthly, within 7 business days after the end of each calendar month.

2. Is there a separate margin account from the trading account? Do I see two sets of accounts when I view my CFD account online?

No, there is only a main trading account. Some CFD providers publish a range of realtime margin values for traders on their online CFD accounts. There is normally one set of accounts, but commonly two pages, one an *account summary page*, the other an *account statement*.

For example, you may see a *margin summary* on the account summary page that includes the account value, the cash amount currently used for margin, the sum available for margin trading, the net exposure of the CFD portfolio and the percentage of exposure that is covered by the account. In addition the percentage of margin utilisation is often shown.

3. If my position goes into loss (requiring, say, another £2000 margin), do I actually get contacted by the CFD provider, or does he just take the money from the funds still remaining in the account?

The CFD provider takes the money required to increase the margin coverage from the existing collateral on the account. If more capital is required, then the provider will contact the client asking them to deposit more margin. Contact will be made by email, via a text message or by phone.

4. Do CFD providers accept anything other than cash to cover margin (e.g. gilts, bonds, equity portfolios)?

Some CFD providers do accept individual stocks, bonds and equity portfolios as well as cash as acceptable margin collateral.

5. Is margin calculated on the bid, offer or mid-price of a share and how often is it calculated?

Margin is normally calculated on the mid-price of a share and it is calculated constantly throughout the trading day. If more margin is required the client will be contacted.

Margin calls

Assessing the correct level of margin in a customer's account depends upon the total open position and the profitability of that position. Customers should be aware of the activity of their open orders so that any movement towards a loss-making situation is recognised. If additional margin is required to bring the NTR back to a positive figure, then a *margin call* will be made by the CFD provider. Once received by the customer, a margin call requires immediate action, although the customer is not obliged to wait for a margin call before attempting to deposit additional funds with the provider to cover the negative exposure of a loss-making position.

Normally, margin calls in excess of £10,000 or €20,000 are due in the form of cleared funds before the end of the same business day so CFD providers will send a message as soon as they can to alert the trader. The trader is then obliged to pay additional funds via bank transfer or credit card to top up the margin account.

Lower margin calls, in the region of £500 or €1000 are communicated in most cases within a few hours by telephone, email or text message (SMS) via a trader's mobile phone in order to alert them.

Margin is illustrated in more detail in the following example.

Example

Assumptions

BP is trading at £5.00 per share; the CFD provider offers the trader a 10% margin facility. A trader uses a proportion of his trading capital to buy 20,000 BP CFDs, depositing £10,000 as initial margin. He pays 0.2% commission.

The following table summarises the fluctuations of the CFD trade as the underlying stock first falls to £4.80 and then rises to £5.20.

	CFD position
Day 1	
Trader equity (£)	10,000
Margin rate	10%
Leverage	10x
Stock price (£)	5.00
CFD purchase	20,000 CFDs
Notional transaction value (£)	100,000
Margin payment (£)	10,000
Commission charged at 0.2% (£)	(200)
Stamp duty (0.5%)	–
Day 5	
Stock price	4.80
Loss to position	4000
Notional transaction value	96,000
Margin call made	4000
Total margin: initial plus variation	14,000
Day 8	
Stock price (£)	5.20
Notional transaction value (£)	104,000
Profit to position (£)	4000
Margin change (£)	8000
Total margin required (£)	*Deposit* + 6000
Day 9	
Stock price (£)	5.20
Closing transaction value (£)	104,000
Profit to position (£)	4000
Commission charged at 0.2% (£)	(240)
Net profit (after commission) (£)	3560 (4000 – 200 – 240)

Margin 10,000 + 4,000   14,000

As can be seen from the example, the trader receives a margin call on Day 5 for additional funds to be deposited in his margin account. Then on Day 8 the trader receives a deposit into his margin account representing the profit he has made on the increased stock price. If the trader decides to close the position for a profit, then he sells the CFD and withdraws the money from his margin account after commissions.

2. Commissions

CFD commissions refer to the charge that a CFD provider will make to a client that buys or sells a CFD. The level of commissions varies between the traded products and the CFD providers with some offering a flat rate irrespective of the trade size and others charging commission as a percentage of the notional value of the trade.

Commissions are often described in terms of basis points (bps) value, that is: the number of ticks that are charged on the transaction. For example, if a CFD provider charges 8bps on both opening and closing CFD trades and the value of the transaction is €10,000, then 8bps would be equivalent to €8.

Minimum commissions

Many CFD providers charge minimum commissions for trading CFDS ranging between, in the UK for example, £5 and £15. Minimum commissions also vary depending on whether the trader is an institutional client or a retail client. Retail clients tend to be charged higher commission rates.

Minimum commissions are chargeable on any size deal so a CFD trader must factor in the potentially high costs associated with smaller transactions. Some CFD providers charge no commission fee for online transactions but a minimum fee of up to £25 for orders delivered by phone.

Some CFD providers do not set minimum commissions but have minimum transaction sizes of 100 CFDs or a minimum notional value of £20,000.

Commission free dealing

Some CFD providers will offer commission-free dealing by incorporating the commission costs into the dealing spread of the CFD bid and offer prices they offer to customers. Although this may look like a good deal, traders should make sure they are fully aware of the cost impact of CFD bid-offer spreads as they can prove to be more expensive than at first thought.

In addition, active CFD traders are often charged reduced commissions compared to less active traders.

Commission Q&A

The table opposite answers some further questions on commission.

Question	Answer
Do commissions payable for transacting CFD orders vary between products?	Yes, actively traded CFDs like stock indices and stocks attract lower commissions than less actively traded products like live cattle. Commissions can be charged as a percentage of the dealing spread or as a flat amount. For example, UK Share CFDs can have a minimum commission of £15 and European shares can have a minimum commission of €25. Both commissions represent a spread of 0.2.
What are the average commissions charged for bonds, stocks, forex and commodities CFDs?	Commissions, on average, range between 0.1%-0.25% of the total consideration of the CFD transaction, long or short, opening or closing.
How do CFD commissions compare to those in the underlying markets?	In most cases in the UK, there is a minimum commission charge for CFD and equity transactions ranging from £5.00-£15.00. Minimum commission charges for CFDs tend to be less than those for equities.
Are commissions charged on a percentage of the trade size or as a fixed rate?	Commissions can be charged in both ways.
If a UK based CFD trader trades a dollar denominated CFD is the commission in US dollars? How is that paid?	The UK based CFD trader will trade in US$ and the commission will be in US$. The CFD provider will set up a US$ account for the trader and will conduct an FX transaction to change the dollars into UK £ when the trader decides to withdraw his funds.
How many times does a CFD trader get charged a commission?	Commissions are normally charged when a CFD position is opened and closed, so there are, in effect, two charges.
If a trader undertakes commission-free dealing is he onto a good thing?	Not necessarily. The commission is wrapped up into the dealing spread so in the example above, the cost of the commission for UK shares is £15 which represents a spread of 0.2. The 0.2 spread for the CFD would be added to the normal 0.5 spread on the underlying making a 0.7 spread in total for the CFD.

3. Financing

A CFD trader with a long position needs to pay interest to fund that position. In effect, the CFD provider is funding the client to hold that position and so the provider charges interest on overnight balances to cover the cost of the funding.

The interest payment (often referred to as the *financing charge*) can be regarded as the *cost of carry* for a position and needs to be factored into the transaction cost as a whole. As financing is charged on a daily basis, interest will not be payable on a position that is opened and closed on the same trading day.

Conversely, traders with short positions receive interest payment from their CFD provider on their overnight short positions.

Quick summary:

- if the CFD position is **long,** then the holder pays interest on the margin account overnight,

- if **short,** the margin account is credited interest.

Long CFD position

A CFD trader buys 5000 Vodafone CFDs with the underlying price at £2.45 (and therefore a notional value of £1600). However, he doesn't have to pay this amount for purchasing the CFDs. In effect, the CFD provider has bought the shares for the trader who borrows the £2450 from the CFD provider. Like borrowing money from a bank, the trader has to pay interest on the loan so he pays the CFD provider interest for the financing facility.

If an open position is held overnight, a finance adjustment is made to the CFD trader's account. This is calculated as follows:

$$d = (n \times p \times i) / t$$

where,

d = daily finance charge

n = number of CFDs traded

p = closing CFD price (usually the mid-price of the underlying share)

i = the relevant overnight LIBOR or LIBID rate (e.g for long positions LIBOR at 2.50% + 2%)

t = 365 (days in the year)

So, in a case where the number of CFDs traded is 5000, the closing price of the underlying share is £2.45 and the LIBOR rate is 2.5% (and the provider's financing debit rate is LIBOR+2%), the overnight debit adjustment to the trading account will be calculated as follows:

(5000 x 2.45 x 4.5%) / 365 = £1.51

Short CFD position

Say a CFD trader sells 5000 Vodafone CFDs short with the underlying price at £2.45 and the LIBID rate is 2.3% (and the provider's financing credit rate is LIBID - 2%), the overnight credit adjustment to the open position will be calculated as follows:

(5000 x 2.45 x 0.3%) / 365 = £0.10

Financing rates

The key question to address now is:

what governs the financing rate charged (or credited) by the CFD provider?

In practice, in the UK, CFD providers tend to use one of the following rates as their reference:

1. Bank of England base rate

2. LIBOR

Having decided on a reference rate (either base rate or LIBOR) CFD providers will then

- charge accounts with overnight **long** positions at the reference rate *plus* a certain amount, and

- credit accounts with overnight **short** positions at the reference rate *minus* a certain amount.

For example, a particular CFD provider may:

- charge accounts with overnight **long** positions at LIBOR + 2%

- credit accounts with overnight **short** positions at LIBID - 2%

Which, if LIBOR is currently at, say, 4.5%, then:

- **long** positions will be charged at a rate of 6.5%, and

- **short** positions will be credited at a rate of 2.5%.

The table opposite gives examples of financing rates for CFD providers at the end of 2008.

Institution	Finance rate
Barclays CFDs	LIBOR +/- 2.5%
Halifax CFDs	LIBOR + 1.5% long LIBOR -2.5% short
City Index	LIBOR +/- 2.5%
CMC Markets	Base rate +/- 3%
GNI Touch	LIBOR +/-3% LIBOR +/- 2.5% for active traders
First Prudential Markets	Reserve bank cash rate +/- 2-3%

As can be seen, most CFD providers reference LIBOR for their financing rates.

LIBOR

A quick word on LIBOR.

Banks lend to each other in the overnight wholesale markets (the *money markets*). The rates at which this lending is done each day are a useful guide to prevailing overnight interest rates. However, there is not just one rate, each transaction between two banks may use a slightly different rate. So, some mechanism was required to determine an average rate.

In 1984 the British Bankers Association devised a system that took all of the overnight interest rates, knocked out the extremes and calculated an average of the rest. It called this average *LIBOR* – which stands for the London Interbank Offer Rate. Today, LIBOR is widely used as a reference for short-term lending rates in different currencies (e.g. GBP, USD, EUR).

However, LIBOR has come under intense scrutiny due to the instability in financial markets that resulted from the seizing up of wholesale money markets. In normal circumstances LIBOR tracks pretty closely the BOE base rate but in July 2007, as the credit crunch started to bite, the two rates diverged (as can be seen in the following chart).

Overnight LIBOR v Base Rate (2007)

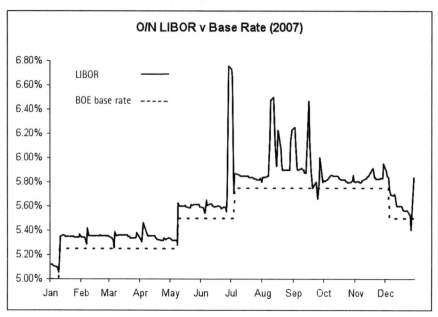

During this time overnight interest charges levied by CFD providers increased substantially; and as CFD traders know, the level of overnight charging has a significant impact on the profitability of CFD trades.

Long-term funding of an open CFD position

As has been seen, CFDs are a very useful short-term trading instrument and there are many advantages to trading CFDs for short periods of time rather than the underlying shares. However, over the longer term, the financing cost of an open CFD position can begin to negate the cost advantages of holding CFDs over shares.

In effect, there is a crossover point in the holding period of a position, beyond which it is better to have held shares rather than CFDs. This crossover point reflects the aggregate costs of share ownership compared to CFDs, which includes share stamp duty and CFD financing costs.

The question is:

how many days will it be before the cost of borrowing funds to finance a CFD open long position outweighs the benefit of missing the stamp duty of 0.5%?

How many days must pass before the cumulative financing costs of the CFD make ownership of the underlying shares more attractive?

The following equation provides a guide:

Stamp duty is levied at 0.5% on the notional value of the underlying instrument so if 12,000 shares are bought at a cost of £1.00 then the stamp duty will be £60.00. If a CFD is bought, no stamp duty is paid, but there is a financing charge of, say, 3% above LIBOR each day that the CFD is open. If LIBOR is at 4% then the open CFD position is costing 7% to finance. Therefore, if the amount borrowed from the CFD provider is £10,000 (the additional £2000 is margin provided by the trader) the cost per day to finance the open CFD position is:

$$0.07 * 10,000/365 = £1.92$$

If the stamp duty benefit of £60 is divided by the cost per day at £1.92, then the cost benefit of owning the CFD over the physical shares ceases after the 31st day. At this point, the CFD has become more expensive to hold than the shares.

Financing currency CFDs

Currency CFDs are treated slightly differently with regard to daily financing, with the daily charge being calculated by using the one-day interest rate differential for the two currencies that make up the open position. The CFD trader receives interest on the currency they have bought and pays interest on the currency they have sold in the currency pair. The conversion of trading costs along with any profits and losses that are incurred is normally based upon the Tom-Next rates, that is, the FX swap rate from tomorrow to the next day, 'tomorrow' meaning the next working day after today and 'next' meaning the day after that.

Financing Q&A

Question	Answer
When interest is debited (for a long position) is it applied to the whole notional value of the position, or the notional value minus the margin that has been put up?	Interest is debited for the whole notional value of the position irrespective of margin.
Similarly, on short positions is interest credited on the whole notional value, or the notional value minus the margin?	The same applies for short positions receiving interest credits on the full notional value of the position.
Is the overnight interest calculated on 360 or 365 day basis? Do all CFD providers use the same method?	Depending on the accounting convention used, interest is charged, or payable, either 360 or 365 days of the year, including weekends. Traditionally, accounting conventions differ between national jurisdictions with the US favouring 360 days and the UK and Europe favouring 365 days. Some CFD providers prefer to stick to these conventions but whichever convention they use is arbitrary.
On short positions is the interest credited referenced to LIBID or LIBOR (and are all CFD providers the same)?	Not all CFD providers are the same, with some using LIBID, LIBOR or the Bank base rate.

4. Tax

While tax treatment for CFDs varies across jurisdictions, broadly speaking any gains (including dividend income and interest payments) made on CFD trading are liable to Capital Gains Tax (CGT). Gains can be offset against losses.

- Dividend income through CFD price adjustments is also charged against CGT.

- Interest payments are also taxable as income.

5. Detailed worked example

The following is a detailed worked example of a CFD trade over four days showing at each stage of the trade process what happens to: the trader's initial cash deposit, the CFD provider's margin requirement, the trader's available capital in his cash account after he places his trade and any changes that occur, the financing charges for carrying the position overnight and the accumulation of losses or profits on the trading account.

Example – a CFD trade in detail

A trader deposits £20,000 into his CFD trading account in anticipation of trading. The money goes directly into his trading account as a cash balance with the CFD provider which is visible to him as a cash deposit on his online account summary page.

He can see the available margin amount that the CFD provider has allocated to him on the same webpage that he is able to see his total account balance.

The trader decides to buy 10,000 CFDs in Barclays Bank (BARC) at a price of £1.50 per CFD. Before he trades, there are some immediate things about BARC that the trader needs to know:

1. BARC is a member of the FTSE 100 Index and as such an opening BARC CFD trade will require margin of 10%.

2. BARC CFDs, like their underlying stock, have a tick value of 0.5 which means that every tick increment movement in the share price is worth £5 per 1000 CFDs.

3. Each BARC CFD will have an initial value of £1.50 to reflect the share price, so 10,000 CFDs will have a notional value of £15,000.

4. The trader starts the day with available leverage of £200,000 (for a FTSE 100 stock) in his CFD account representing a margin availability from his provider of ten times his lodged capital of £20,000.

5. With a 10% margin requirement for BARC, the trader will need to pay an initial margin amount of £1500 when buying 10,000 BARC CFDs.

6. The CFD provider will pay interest on a positive end of day balance of over £20,000.

7. The CFD provider charges a commission of 0.2% of the notional value of the purchased CFD.

As can be seen from the following table, on Day 1 the trader starts out with £20,000 in his trading account. The cash account is reduced by £1500 plus the commission charge of 0.2% by buying 10,000 CFDs. The CFD provider debits margin of £1500 initially from his trading account, but the amount of margin required over time will vary depending on whether the share price goes up or down. If the price of BARC goes down, the trader's trading account will be debited more cash in the way of variation margin. If the price of BARC shares goes up, the trading account will be credited.

Day 1

Trader's initial cash account deposit	£20,000
Leverage allocated by CFD provider	£200,000
Action	Buy 10,000 BARC CFDs
BARC share price	£1.50
Notional value of CFD trade	£15,000
Commission charged at 0.2%	£30
Margin deposit (10%)	£1500
Unrealised profit/loss	0
End balance left in account	£18,470

The trader holds the long CFD position overnight, and is charged interest on the notional value of his open position at LIBOR + 2%. This amount is debited from his trading account.

Overnight finance charge

Trader's initial cash account deposit	£20,000
Open position	Long 10,000 BARC CFDs
BARC share price at close of business	£1.50
Overnight charge on notional value of position	LIBOR (4%) + 2% = 6%
Total charge for overnight position	(10,000 x 1.5 x 6%)/365 = £2.46
Non-attributed cash value left in trading account	£18,470 - £2.46 = 18,467.54

Day 2

On Day 2, the BARC share price falls by 10p and the loss to the CFD position of £1000 is reflected in a reduction in the value of the trader's cash account as well as variation margin of £1000.

Trader's initial cash account deposit	£20,000
Open Position	Long 10,000 BARC CFDs
BARC share price at close of business	£1.40
Notional value of CFD Trade	£14,000
Variation margin required	£1500 + £1000 = £2500
Overnight charge on notional value of position	LIBOR + 2% = 6%
Total charge for overnight position	(10,000 x 1.4 x 6%)/365 = £2.30
Non-attributed cash value left in trading account	£18,467.54 - £1000 - £1000 - £2.30 = £16,465.24

Day 3

On Day 3 the BARC share price falls again and closes at £1.30. The trader is again charged variation margin of a further £1000 and incurs another £1000 reduction in his cash account.

Trader's initial cash account deposit	£20,000
Open position	Long 10,000 BARC CFDs
BARC share price at close of business	£1.30
Notional value of CFD trade	£13,000
Variation margin required	£2500 + £1000 = £3500
Overnight charge on notional value of position	LIBOR + 2% = 6%
Total charge for overnight position	(10,000 x 1.3 x 6%)/365 = £2.13
Non-attributed cash value left in trading account	£16,465.24 - £1000 - £1000 - 2.13 = £14,463.11

Day 4

On Day 4 the BARC share price shows no letting up as it falls to £1.25 and the trader decides to sell the CFDs so as not to incur further losses. The trade is closed out for a 0.2% fee.

Summary table: outcome of the trade

	Day 1	Day 2	Day 3	Day 4
Trader's initial deposit	£20,000			
Action/position	Buy 10,000 BARC CFDs	Long 10,000 BARC CFDs	Long 10,000 BARC CFDs	Sell 10,000 BARC CFDs
BARC share price	£1.50	£1.40	£1.30	£1.25
Notional value of CFD position	£15,000	£14,000	£13,000	£12,500
Commission charged at 0.2%	£30			£25
Financing charge overnight	0	£2.46	£2.30	£2.13
Margin level	-£1500	-£2500	-£3500	+£3500
Unrealised loss/profit	0	-£1000	-£2000	-£2500
End balance in account	£18,470	£16,467.54	£14,465.24	£17,438.11

Summary

The realised loss to the position is £2500 with the total trade costs being £61.89. The trader's cash account is now valued at £17,438.11, a reduction of over 12.5% of the trader's starting capital of £20,000 four days earlier.

Equity CFDs and corporate actions

The holder of an open position in equity CFDs should be aware of the types of corporate actions that can affect their position. This section covers:

- shareholders rights,

- dividend payments and capital adjustments,

- capital raising (rights issues), and

- mergers.

Shareholder rights

Taking a long position in an equity CFD does not mean that the trader has the same rights of ownership as a holder of the shares. Only under (rare) pre-arranged circumstances is the CFD exchangeable for the underlying security or its benefits, as is the case with stock options or stock futures upon expiration, exercise or assignment.

Although the price movement in the CFD is equal to that of the underlying instrument, the CFD is a completely separate entity and remains an over-the-counter (OTC) agreement between a CFD provider and the trader. As such, the rights accruing to owners of the underlying security do not translate to the holder of a CFD.

CFD holders therefore have no shareholder rights.

They have no voting rights or other rights associated with share ownership – this is the reason why they don't have to pay stamp duty. They do not receive a share certificate, but they do, however, participate in corporate events like share dividends, rights issues and stock adjustments [discussed further below].

As a CFD position reflects the exposure of either a purchaser or seller of shares in an underlying company, it will also reflect any capital adjustments or benefits announced by the company. Therefore:

> Owners of CFDs will partake in corporate actions but are not entitled to any voting rights.

Dividend payments

CFD traders are subject to different rules with regard to dividend payments compared to traders who hold the physical stock.

Companies pay dividends to shareholders at regular periods during the year, this might be annually, half yearly or quarterly depending on the company's reporting period.

There are three key dates to be aware of regarding dividends:

1. *announcement date*: the day the company announces the details of the dividend (the details include the amount of the dividend and the timing of the ex-div and payment dates)

2. *ex-div date*: holders of the shares up to this date are entitled to the dividend (a trader can sell the shares after the ex-div date and will still receive the dividend)

3. *payment date*: the day on which the dividend is actually paid (the payment date can be several weeks after the ex-div date)

Normally, dividends are announced by the company with a given ex-dividend date and a payment date, meaning that a certain time elapses between the date the dividend is announced, the date it is awarded to holders of the stock, and the date the dividend is physically paid.

Example: trader holds physical shares

A trader holds 10,000 shares of BP and the company announces a half yearly dividend of 20p per share. At this time of the dividend announcement, the company also announces the ex-div date and the payment date.

On the *ex-div date*, the price of the underlying share will drop by the amount of the dividend to reflect the value of the dividend, For example, if BP share price is £5.00 and the dividend is 20p, then the share price will drop to £4.80 on ex-div day.

On *payment date*, the trader will receive £2000 (that is, 20p x 10,000 shares).

Example: trader holds CFDs

A trader that holds a long open CFD position in the stock on its ex-div date will be credited a dividend adjustment equal to 90% of the net dividend awarded to shareholders.

If the CFD trader has a short open position, they will incur a charge for the dividend adjustment equal to 100% of the net dividend awarded to stock holders.

Withholding tax in the UK

The reason for the difference between the two price adjustments, the long being 90% and the short being 100%, is due to the witholding tax implications of receiving dividend incomes.

UK company dividends are paid net of 10% witholding tax. The present rate of the UK tax for gross dividend income is 32.5% for higher rate earners and 10% for lower rate earners. The witholding tax lower rate of 10% deducted at source on UK dividend payments is viewed by the Inland Revenue as a tax credit so earners whose income falls below the UK income tax threshold of £37,400 for 2009-2010 do not have to pay additional income tax on their dividend income. It is this lower rate of witholding tax at 10% that is reflected in the long CFD dividend payment adjustment of 90%.

The short CFD holder is liable to pay the entire 100% of the dividend, however, because of the immediate share price adjustment of 100% of the value of the dividend on ex-div day. As the short CFD holder is expected to pay the dividend adjustment on ex-div day, the dividend adjustment must be 100% of the dividend reflected in the reduced share price.

Paying tax on UK dividend income

Tax is paid at 32.5% on UK dividend income depending on the tax allowance threshold of the individual.

- **If you pay tax at the basic rate** you have no additional tax to pay on your dividend income because the tax liability is 10 per cent – the same amount as the Witholding tax credit deducted at source.

- **If you pay tax at the higher rate** you pay a total of 32.5% tax on dividend income that exceeds the basic rate income tax limit (£37,400 for the 2009-10 tax year). But because the first 10% of the tax due on your dividend income is already covered by the witholding tax credit, in practice you owe 22.5%.

However, for CFD traders there is an important difference: holders of the stock over the ex-div date receive a dividend payment that is treated as income by the Inland Revenue. However, the holder of the CFD receives a positive price adjustment which is treated as a capital gain. This could have capital gains tax implications for CFD traders who participate in trading strategies that involve dividends over the ex-dividend date.

One advantage the CFD holder has over the equity holder is that they receive the dividend adjustment on the ex-dividend date, while the holder of the underlying stock receives their dividend payment on the payment date, which can be up to a few months after the ex-dividend date. Other corporate actions like rights issues, scrips and stock bonuses are also paid on the ex-date to a holder of CFDs.

Example: dividends

The following table summarises the effect of a 30p dividend paid by BP to traders who are long and short of stock and CFDs.

	Long stock	Short stock	Long CFD	Short CFD
Open position (£)	10,000	-10,000	10,000	-10,000
19 Dec 2007 30p dividend announced				
20 Feb 2008 Ex-dividend date	Stock price falls by dividend amount. Holders of long stock guaranteed dividend payment on payment date.	Stock price falls by dividend amount. Traders short of stock must pay dividend on payment date.	90% dividend received by way of CFD price adjustment.	100% dividend payable by way of CFD Price adjustment.
2 Apr 2008 payment date	100% dividend payment received net after withholding tax	100% of dividend payable		

Capital raising and bonus issues

Companies list on a stock exchange in order to raise money and may revisit the market for funding several times. Such capital raising often takes the form of rights issues, which can present the CFD trader with interesting trading opportunities (as described in the chapter titled 'CFD Trading Strategies').

Rights issues

When a company launches a rights issue it is a capital-raising exercise. The company offers new shares to existing shareholders in proportion to their current shareholding, usually at a discount to the current share price. The shareholder then has a choice to either take up the rights in full or sell the rights into the market (known as nil paid rights).

CFD traders with long positions will receive the benefits of rights issues in the same way that holders of the physical stock do. They may also be offered the option of whether to participate in the rights issue or not, whereas CFD traders who are short CFDs do not have the same option and may be assigned a short position following the ex-rights date.

During rights issues the stock price can become more volatile which provides trading opportunities for CFD traders. The rights shares themselves are tradable before the ex-rights date [an example of a trading strategy is given in the Strategies chapter]. After the ex-rights date the rights shares cease trading and a single share price with the factored-in rights price resumes.

A flaw in the current UK rights issue rules is that the procedure takes so long compared with, for example, the US. For example, Lehman Brothers announced their capital raising initiative on 9 June 2008 and alerted the press on the morning of the 12 June 2008 that it had been completed. It is not the same in the UK. HBOS had to wait from 22 April to 8 June to see its capital raising process completed. This flaw, however, enables the UK CFD trader to benefit from rights issue volatility.

Bonus issues

A bonus issue (often referred to as a scrip issue or stock split) is a corporate action whereby a company will issue new shares in addition to existing shares. This results in an increase in the number of shares in circulation accompanied by a pro-rata reduction in the share price so that after the bonus issue the value of any holding in the shares remains the same even if there are more shares in issue.

Bonus issues, rights issues and stock splits will be replicated in the CFD on the corresponding ex-date. On ex-date client positions will be adjusted to allow for the effect of the corporate action on the market price.

Mergers and mergers with elections

For mandatory mergers CFD holders are paid cash or new CFDs on the ex-event date. CFD holders do not have the right to vote on mergers with elections. CFD traders with short positions will be debited, and those with long positions credited, in the same way that holders or short sellers of physical stock are.

3

Managing a CFD Account

This chapter deals with the logistics of choosing a CFD provider, opening and managing a CFD account and trading with the provider's software.

I have taken the UK provider as an example in most cases, although the same logistical procedures could be applied to other global providers.

Opening an account

As a preliminary to opening a CFD account with any provider you will need to know:

- What kind of trader you are

- If the CFD provider is a market maker or agency broker

- The history of the CFD provider and their degree of solvency

- The quality of the trading software provided

- What research is provided

- What other support services are provided (e.g. educational seminars and 24-hour help desks)

Choosing a CFD provider

How do CFD providers differ or are all CFD providers the same?

CFD providers are definitely not the same, but in the main the differences are in matters of detail rather than any significant differences in types of service provided. Differences may be seen in terms of the level of commission charges, the quality of trading software, or the quality of trade support and research.

CFD traders can choose a CFD provider that offers them the level of service they require – be it the top of the range full brokerage services or bottom of the range execution only services. Occasionally CFD traders may have accounts with more than one CFD provider depending on how their trading activity changes and what demands they have.

Brokers and market makers

As mentioned in Chapter 2, there are two kinds of provider in general: the agency broker and the market maker, and both have different ways of charging for their trading services. The broker charges a dealing commission and the market maker charges via the dealing spread. Some CFD traders prefer the broker because the fees are known and the transaction takes place at the price on the underlying market via DMA. Market makers, however, can adjust the dealing spreads to suit their trading books so there is seldom a set dealing spread. However, market makers make their own liquidity, if underlying markets are thinly traded, a CFD market maker may provide a bid-offer spread of greater size for a client.

Criteria for selecting a provider

In addition to the range of products available to trade and the liquidity pool that the CFD provider is likely to provide access to, there are several other important aspects of a CFD provider's services that customers should consider when deciding which provider to choose. For example–

- Which CFD provider offers the best opportunity for margined trading and the most cost-effective policy relating to transaction fees, interest charges, and account management fees (see below)?

- Which CFD provider offers the best trading software and technical support?

- Is the potential CFD provider a white label provider of CFD trading services and, if so, what additional costs are incurred because of this arrangement?

- How is market data provided by the CFD provider? Is there a separate charge for this?

- Does the CFD provider offer value-added services like economic news, technical analysis and economic research?

- Does the CFD provider have a good range of permitted order types?

- Does the CFD provider have an in-house educational programme?

Many of the services mentioned above are offered by individual CFD providers, but there are subtle differences in the approaches that some providers take. In particular, there is a difference in the way that customer orders are handled by broker intermediaries and market makers. In addition, charges for accessing market data can vary and the range of premium services can also differ. A newcomer to the CFD marketplace should spend time researching the different types of service provided by a range of CFD providers before signing up with one as a customer.

CFD providers are constantly searching for new and useful value added services to offer their customers. Those on offer currently include:

- charting and technical analysis provided through applications embedded in the CFD provider's front-end trading platform,

- company research facilities, normally provided via website access,

- economic forecasting and news updates; and

- online and classroom-based educational programmes.

Account management fees and referral commissions

It is also a good idea to check the small print of the contract with a CFD provider for details of the account management fees that CFD providers may charge. Some CFD providers charge for the following services, which can cause some surprises for CFD traders who don't expect them:

- charges for order changes, amendments and cancellations

- a margin call fee

- fees for execution of wire transfers

- fees for printing and posting of reports on trading activities

- fees for answering queries from accountants regarding a client's trading account

Some employees of CFD providers are remunerated via commissions for services they provide to CFD trading clients. Where a third party refers a CFD trader's business there are often commissions paid for doing so. It is worth checking how the employees and third parties are likely to be remunerated and if this cost will affect trading costs directly or indirectly.

What kind of trader are you?

Before decisions can be made as to the choice of CFD provider, one of the preliminary considerations for a trader is what kind of trader he or she is.

Active trader

If the trader is an active CFD trader with a broad trading remit covering several different markets, then there are two choices:

1. The first option will be to enter into an agreement with a **market maker**. CFD market makers tend to have an advantage when it comes to the spectrum of instruments they can trade because, unlike CFD agent brokers, they are not reliant upon underlying instrument liquidity in order to provide tradable quotes. If a stock is illiquid in the underlying market, a market maker may decide to make a more liquid market in CFDs due to his ability to lay off risk with other instruments. This is an advantage for market makers as illiquid instruments will be subject to wider dealing spreads and therefore can be more profitable to trade.

2. The second option for the CFD trader is to find a **provider who specialises** in the types of products that he wishes to trade and who offers DMA (Direct Market Access), so that he can participate in the bid-offer spread of the underlying instrument.

Less active trader

If the trader is less active, they may be better electing for a limited risk trading service, whereby they are covered should the market behave adversely.

Opening a CFD trading account

As mentioned above, before opening a CFD trading account it is advisable to research several important aspects of the CFD provider's service. Opening a CFD trading account requires that the trader has good knowledge of:

- his **customer type** classification

- his **money management** requirements

- the **account application** process

- any **operational risks**

[I have taken examples from UK CFD providers for the next section, although as I mentioned earlier in the chapter the same procedures apply to CFD providers from other countries.]

Customer type

Due to the nature of CFDs, financial regulators may require special controls, such as the classification of clients.

In the UK, the Financial Services Authority (FSA) recommends the classifying of clients into the following categories:

1. **Private customers** are less sophisticated traders who are accordingly afforded the greatest degree of regulatory protection.

2. **Intermediate customers** are more experienced traders and they will generally either have appropriate expertise in-house, or will have the means to pay for professional advice if this is needed.

These categories apply equally to instruments like futures and options, as well as CFDs. CFD providers categorise new customers according to the information they provide in new account applications. The assignation of either private or intermediate status means very different things with regard to the type of service the customer can expect from their CFD provider.

1. Private customers

Private customers can expect to receive the benefit of full FSA protection. Less experienced traders fall into this category and may require assistance in managing their risk exposure and trading activities.

2. Intermediate customers

Intermediate customers have to accept a reduced service from the CFD provider, in respect of:

- rules governing the issuing of direct offer financial promotions;

- ensuring that customers understand the nature of the risks they are undertaking;

- the provider's obligation to disclose their charges;

- the way in which they remunerate third party introducing entities, along with the commission they either receive or pay;

- financing arrangements, with details of the restrictions on lending money or providing credit to private customers;

- margin management processes with details of the circumstances in which a customer may be required to provide additional margin; and

- the process by which customers are offered OTC traded instruments and how they are competitively priced.

An important point to consider is that intermediate customers do not have the automatic right to receive best execution in all the instruments they trade, and their written consent is not required by the provider for certain custody arrangements.

As a result of classification as an intermediate customer, any money received from the customer, or held by a CFD provider on their behalf, will not (unless otherwise agreed in writing) be subject to the protection conferred by the FSA's client money rules. As a consequence of this, the intermediate customer's money is not segregated from the CFD provider's own money and may be used by the provider in the course of undertaking its own business. In this respect, intermediate customers are effectively *general creditors* of the CFD provider and will be treated as such if the CFD provider becomes insolvent.

Financial Ombudsman Service (FOS)

In addition, an intermediate customer does not have the same rights of access to the Financial Ombudsman Service (FOS) as a private customer. The FOS was established as a result of the Financial Services and Markets Act of 2000, and aims to resolve disputes between financial services firms and their clients in an expeditious and less formal way. As part of this initiative, CFD providers must ensure that any written or verbal communication with all their clients is clearly stated, fair and not misleading.

Account type

Before the trader has made a decision with regard to the most appropriate CFD provider, it is vital that they select the right account type for their particular trading and investment needs. Trading accounts can be set up with CFD providers for individuals, joint partnerships and corporate users. There are typically four types of account:

1. execution only

2. discretionary

3. advisory

4. limited risk

In order to make an informed choice with regard to the right trading account for the customer, the CFD provider will assess the information they provide via the account application and will then recommend one of the following accounts.

1. Execution only accounts

Execution only accounts are suitable for experienced traders who do not require advice or trading recommendations from the CFD provider. Traders with several years of experience and a track record of profitable trading will not necessarily require the CFD provider to offer them additional services, but will use the provider's trading application and order routing network to trade directly in the market, making their own decisions with regard to trading strategies.

2. Discretionary accounts

Discretionary accounts enable the CFD provider to trade on behalf of the customer using the customer's deposited funds. The customer is able to set certain limits with regard to risk and acceptable loss, but these are only guidelines and are not strictly enforced.

Using a discretionary trading service may seem to be an acceptable and useful service for a private customer who does not have the same degree of trading expertise as the CFD provider, or the time to devote to the endeavour. However, in the course of trading on behalf of the discretionary account holder, any losses incurred by the provider are applied directly to the customer's account. This means that discretionary account holders are subject to the same risks as other account holders but are not directly involved in the day-to-day management of their account. As long as discretionary account customers are willing to accept the risks associated with this trading service, they can benefit from the account manager's expertise with regard to investment strategy.

3. Advisory accounts

Advisory trading accounts are only offered to those customers who can be categorised as intermediate. The CFD provider provides a full suite of advisory services and offers trading ideas and trade management directly applicable to the customer's open positions. While the CFD provider offers expertise and insight into trading opportunities, it is the responsibility of the customer to decide whether the advice is suitable for them. As mentioned earlier, an intermediate customer signs away certain rights under FSA regulations that would be applicable to private customers, and the degree of autonomy that a customer requires is in direct relation to the level of protection he receives.

4. Limited risk accounts

Private customers who require an automatic element of risk control can establish a risk control arrangement with the CFD provider through a limited risk account. The objective with the limited liability orders that form part of this arrangement is to provide the trader with a limited liability stop loss element when he opens his long trading position.

A premium (of between 0.75% and 1% of the traded amount) for this limited liability provision is payable immediately the position is opened and certain other conditions are levied on the service. For example, some CFD providers will only provide limited liability options on leading large cap stocks, like those in the FTSE 100 Index or the DAX Index; and then the stop has to be at least 5% away from the current tradable price. Even with the 5% provision, there is no guarantee that the limited liability stop will be executed at exactly the price at which it has been set, although in most cases CFD providers will honour their obligations to limited risk account customers.

Some stock price movements can be very volatile. For example, in late 2007 Rio Tinto Zinc (RTZ) received a bid approach from BHP Billiton. The RTZ price moved £10 with minimal trading volume in a matter of milliseconds. Given the volatility in the RTZ stock prior to the bid announcement and the sudden increase in volatility seen in the RTZ traded options premiums, indications were that there was a likelihood of a sudden change in the RTZ share price. CFD providers would have been reluctant to have written guaranteed stop loss CFDs against the stock given these conditions.

White label providers

Several CFD providers allow third party financial institutions to white label their trading software and transaction services so that customers of these institutions can trade CFDs with them. This is a common practice and is not intended to deceive the customer.

There are good reasons for financial institutions not wanting to design and build their own versions of CFD trading software, and customers should not be put off opening trading accounts with institutions that offer third party trading applications. CFD providers make it their business to specialise in CFD trading services, while other financial institutions, such as banks, do not. As a result, a bank may not want to spend money and time recreating what is already available in the way of third party CFD trading software, but would rather use a CFD provider's expertise and already-available trading platform.

If a financial institution, such as a bank, starts offering CFD trading services to its customers, those customers may want reassurance that the third party provider the bank is sanctioning to provide these services is capable of doing so. By offering a white label version of a third party CFD trading application, the bank is putting its stamp on the services that that provider is offering and therefore it must manage its relationship with the CFD provider very carefully. While financial institutions may not make it readily apparent who they are using as third party providers, customers can make their own enquiries with regard to the relationship between the two institutions.

The types of third party CFD trading services adopted by financial institutions may differ. If a white label CFD provider is a market maker, then the bank or client institution may make money from its customer order flow by taking a small increment in the dealing spread from the market maker. On the other hand, client institutions may charge a customer an additional commission for the service.

With regard to the technicalities of white label services, there are a couple of approaches:

1. Customer orders may be sent via the third party white labelled trading software to the bank's own internal servers and then via a DNS alias (that

is, the order is rerouted to a destination host server run by the third party CFD provider) to the CFD provider for order management and transaction. The financial institution's objective is to hide the fact that a third party is managing the CFD transaction services.

2. A financial institution may just require the third party provider's front-end trading system, matching the orders sent from customers via that system on its own internal servers.

While there are differences in the two approaches, as long as the trading service is of an acceptable standard and the charges are not unreasonable, it should not make a difference to the customer which of the two methods an institution uses.

Mark-ups and spread differences

While there are few reasons for doubting the efficiency of a white labelled CFD trading application provided by a financial institution to its customers, those customers who decide to open CFD trading accounts knowing that the bank has a third party white label arrangement with a CFD provider should make themselves aware of the bank's charging structure.

In the third party arrangement between the bank and the CFD provider, the CFD provider makes the CFD bid-offer spread available to the bank's customers, who then trade through the white labelled trading application with the CFD provider, *not* the bank.

How then does the bank profit from the relationship?

The short answer is through manipulation of the charges or dealing spread.

Financial institutions using third party white label CFD trading applications are able to alter the charges they apply to customer orders in two ways:

1. By marking up a charge through widening the bid-offer dealing spread they offer to clients.

2. By changing the dealing price after a CFD trade has been transacted but before reporting it to customers.

Following Financial Services Authority (FSA) rules, the bank would be required to announce its charging structure to customers before they sign trading agreements. Once the charging structure has been made known, the bank could add up to 0.1% to the client's CFD trading spread for its own profitability.

Bid-offer spreads can be changed by CFD providers to reflect the types of customer that are dealing. For example, the spread difference for an institutional customer can be half that of a retail customer. The bank could choose to receive half of the spread differential.

Market maker or agency broker?

Whether to choose a market maker CFD provider to trade with or a broker counterparty CFD provider depends upon your trading criteria. Both have different business models.

A CFD market maker in Deutsche Bank shares, for example, will quote a dealing spread (that is, a bid and an offer price) based on the underlying share price quoted on Xetra but is not obliged to copy it. The market maker's quoted price depends on other factors internal to his dealing operation.

On the other hand, the CFD broker passes on the exact share price that is quoted on the exchange by writing the CFD contract with the trader in direct correlation. So if the trader buys 2000 Deutsche Bank CFDs, the offer price that is quoted on Xetra is the price that he pays for the CFD. The CFD broker writes the trader a CFD contract while simultaneously hedging himself through the purchase of the shares.

The market maker, however, may want to go on risk by writing the CFD contract for the trader but without fully hedging the position with the underlying share. A broker doesn't have the same opportunity as a market maker to take a long or short position like this as the broker will match the terms of the CFD contract like for like with the underlying instrument via DMA.

In addition, market makers are able to improve upon the listed underlying price with their own quotation if it suits their trading book, whereas brokers will match the best bid-offer spread in the underlying cash market. Some CFD traders prefer to trade with a market maker as counterparty as they can sometimes enjoy tighter best bid-offer spreads.

The only potential drawback is that the market maker can elect to withdraw his quotation or reduce his available dealing sizes at any time if market volatility increases suddenly or the quotation doesn't suit his book. The broker, on the other hand, will stand by the quotation in the underlying security as long as he can get his hedge on. So, if there are 2000 BMW shares on XETRA on offer at €30.50 then a CFD order up to 2000 at that price is tradable as long as the offer remains in place while the order is being executed.

It may not be as crucial for a new CFD trader to select one type of CFD trader over another as it is for a more seasoned CFD trader who trades more frequently and expects a particular type of service. The new CFD trader will need to understand his trading style more fully before selecting the CFD provider that truly suits his needs so experimenting with both types of provider could be advantageous in the initial stages.

CFD provider solvency

New customers opening an account with a CFD provider need to be aware of the risks involved in this arrangement. Unlike when dealing through, say, a stockbroker, a trader transacts with an OTC CFD provider on a principal-to-principal basis – not an agency basis. So, the trader has exposure to the credit risk of the CFD provider.

The continued solvency of the CFD provider is therefore of major importance and new customers must exercise due diligence in studying the disclosure obligations, credit ratings, trading track record and general financial information of the provider. This information can sometimes be difficult to find but CFD providers are normally open to answering such questions for new customers. In fact, they often provide seminars for new traders and answer a number of the questions there. In addition, traders can often get access to corporate documents on CFD provider's websites that answer many of these questions.

CFD provider compulsory closure

The CFD provider also has risk. If a customer cannot make a margin call, for example, then the provider has the authority to close out the open position by way of compulsory closure. Although this is not a preferred alternative to securing margin, it nonetheless demonstrates the need for CFD providers to ascertain the ongoing credit worthiness of their clients.

As margin is calculated daily on a mark-to-market basis, any inability to cover a shortfall may result in the position being closed at the prevailing market price. This can result in a loss that the CFD trader may or may not be able to pay. Whether or not to close a position is at the discretion of the CFD provider, even if the customer does not agree with the action.

Corporate takeovers

Other examples of events that may lead to compulsory closure of CFD open positions include corporate actions in the underlying instrument. In the case of a takeover bid for the associated company, the open CFD position will usually be closed out at the prevailing market price one day prior to the last day the shares were quoted in their existing form.

Account application process

When applying for a CFD account new customers may be asked to follow the three stage process outlined below.

1. Send an initial account opening deposit

When a new CFD account is opened it must be funded with an *initial deposit*. Initial deposit levels required by CFD providers differ in their amounts required and the currency they accept. It is not uncommon for some CFD providers to require US dollar deposits and to manage a client's trading account in US dollars, even if the trader is domiciled in the UK or Europe. As such, all non US currency deposits are rebased to US dollars until they are drawn by the client.

CFD providers often have minimum cash levels they expect new clients to deposit. These levels can range from a zero balance requirement up to £20,000 depending on the type of client. Other deposit levels of £200, £500, £1000 or £5000 are not uncommon. Providers may also accept share portfolios as collateral for a start-up CFD trading account, or a combination of share portfolios and cash.

Ongoing, there are several ways that traders can fund a CFD trading account. They can: write a cheque drawn on a UK clearing bank; provide a bank guarantee; send funds via bank wire transfer; or pay by credit or debit card. UK clearing bank cheques can take up to 10 days to clear and foreign clearing bank cheques can take considerably longer. There is normally a charge of 1.5% levied by the CFD provider for money sent from a credit card company to cover administrative costs, and charges levied by the card company. In addition, the credit card company may treat credit card payments made to a CFD provider as cash advances, which will then incur extra charges and interest. It is important that traders research the likely costs associated with using a credit card to fund a CFD trading account.

Another point to remember is that CFD providers will not accept cheques from third parties whose names do not match the name of the trading account. This is primarily to limit the likelihood of money laundering. Furthermore, the following cash or cash equivalents may not be accepted: post office money orders, cashier's cheques, traveller's cheques or bankers' drafts.

2. Download the CFD provider's front-end trading software

The CFD provider will require new customers to register with them as new account holders and to activate the trading software so that usernames, passwords and account numbers can be verified and initialised. CFD software trading applications fall into two main categories: thick and thin–

- *Thin clients* ("client" in this context just means a software program running on a PC) are lightweight in terms of their memory and database requirements, with the actual software trading application likely to be hosted on the CFD provider's computer system rather than on the customer's computer. The lighter component of the client front-end trading application resides on the PC of the trader, with the heavier number-crunching part of the application being hosted at the provider's end.

- *Thick clients* are different, in that the main part of the application is hosted on the trader's PC rather than on the CFD provider's computer. This means that traders will need to have suitably robust PCs to be able to satisfy the memory and database requirements of the software.

Web-based trading applications are normally quite light being in the range of 6-10Mb. Some CFD providers offer larger thick client versions weighing in at 40% more than that however; the larger versions normally have more functionality which can be useful for traders. The type of trading platform that the new trader accesses depends on the sophistication of his trading so it is important that the trader discusses this with the provider before opting for a particular service.

3. Wait for notification from the provider that the account is open

The CFD provider is likely to take 24-48 hours to assess the application and to verify the account and personal information that the applicant has supplied. The checks that they perform are rigorous and detailed. CFD providers are very wary of money laundering scams, whereby accounts are opened fraudulently and trading is undertaken merely to facilitate the money laundering process.

Once the account is opened

Once the trading account is operational the customer should quickly gain a firm understanding of the trading account management requirements. They will be required to manage their accounts efficiently and responsibly, understanding how to fund an account, maintain appropriate margin, reconcile open positions with risk expectations, understand the way that interest is charged and is payable, and understand the fee structure of the account.

Contact between CFD provider and customer

The frequency with which customers are contacted by their CFD provider depends upon the level of service they have. The active CFD trader will naturally be in contact with the CFD provider more often than the inactive trader, mainly because of the demands of managing the trading account.

The CFD provider is likely to want to relay transaction and margin information to the active CFD trader at regular intervals and may do this via email, phone calls or texting to the customer using Short Message Service (SMS) via a mobile phone.

Inactive traders may receive information concerning margin calls via telephone, or via letter the next business day depending on how much margin is required.

Research

Most CFD providers offer some form of research capability either from in-house researchers or from third party research companies.

In-house seminars and education programmes

Conducting educational programmes for new and existing customers has benefits for traders and providers alike. Newcomers to the market receive valuable training in tradable products, market technology, strategy selection and the nuances of market behaviour, while the CFD provider gains useful knowledge of the potential trading abilities of the new customers. Those customers that attend in-house educational programmes are often given the opportunity to test-drive the trading software with play money and can spend several hours trading on simulated markets. This helps the customer get to grips with the trading software and the product itself.

FSA compliance

There are several compliance documents and processes that a CFD trader should be familiar with when trading CFDS. They are:

- The CFD provider's **Risk warning letter** – this details all the risks associated with trading CFDs.

- The **terms and conditions** for trading – the idea is that the CFD trader and provider enter into a two-way agreement in respect of the terms and conditions document so that both parties understand their obligations.

- The **conduct of business rules.**

- The regulations governing **account segregation** – the CFD provider is required to hold client's money in segregated accounts in accordance with the regulations of the FSA, but, as described elsewhere, with regard to third party insolvency, this may not provide the basis for complete protection of those funds, with only a proportion of them being repayable following insolvency.

Third party solvency

One of the major risks for CFD traders is the potential insolvency of the CFD provider. Insolvency (or default) of the third party responsible for writing OTC CFDs may lead to all open positions being liquidated or closed out without the consent of the CFD client. Although, with CFD market makers, for example, the practice of order book risk management through hedging is an ongoing exercise, customers must not expect to get all their money back if an unexpected event occurs that pushes the CFD provider into insolvency. In 2008, a victim of such an event was Global Trader Europe, a CFD provider.

The consequences of the insolvency of a CFD provider in the UK are:

- You may not get back the assets you lodged as collateral and, instead, may be offered an alternative cash payment.

- You will be covered for deposits up to £50,000 by the Financial Services Compensation Scheme and investments to a maximum of £48,000 (the first £30,000 is paid in full, with 90% of the remaining balance being payable to a total of £48,000).

- This compensation scheme does not apply to intermediate customers of CFD providers.

CFD trading software

Web-based order, trade and account management services provided by CFD agent brokers and market makers through their proprietary trading software have become increasingly sophisticated and progressively user-friendly over the past ten years, reflecting the increased sophistication of market participants. The quality and stability of the front-end trading platform is a major consideration for CFD traders, and CFD providers spend a great deal of money and time each year on improving network communications, software functionality and customer support services.

Each CFD provider has its own trading software, and several of them receive awards each year for the ingenuity and excellence of their products. A CFD provider's trading software will differentiate it from the rest of the marketplace so a great deal of thought goes into software upgrades and branding.

Testing the trading program

It is a good idea to test a CFD provider's trading program. The software can usually be downloaded from the providers' websites, or sent by post on a CD once a demo or live trading account has been opened.

In some cases, the CFD account does not need to be fully funded until a demo version of the software has been tried out; although it is in the best interests of the CFD provider to get the customer to trade as soon as possible, and demo account management is geared towards getting the customer to make his first live trade.

In some instances, CFD provider's client software applications can be loaded onto more than one computer using the same user ID and password. This means that if a customer wants to load the trading software onto their laptop computer but also wants the application to be available on their desktop PC. This can be done by copying the original software access encryption key from the PC to the laptop. The requirements for setting this up are specific to each CFD provider so traders would need to check the procedures with their own providers.

Most CFD providers offer free trial periods to new customers. These range from a few days to a few weeks and enable the customer to test out the trading software services with play money before they commit to opening an account.

The CFD provider's objective is to get the customer to trade as quickly as possible, but the trader should take the time required to understand the software application and feel comfortable with it.

Some CFD providers do not offer free trials, however, and customers open accounts on the live version of the trading software from the outset. This can be a little daunting for some customers if they are new to online trading. The sensible approach is to use the demonstration software to paper trade and to contact the CFD provider if there are any problems or questions. One thing to remember is that it is not in the interest of the CFD provider to see a customer lose his equity through adopting poor trading habits, so many providers offer educational resources to help customers acquire good trading habits and to understand the instruments and markets they are trading.

The following table provides tips and suggestions for a trader to consider when testing new software.

Trading software checklist

Question	Answer
Is the software easily navigable with a mouse or keyboard and do the component parts fit together well?	CFD traders do not want to spend time trying to figure out how to navigate the software when they should be trading.
Does the software require any additional hardware or software than currently exists on your PC?	Most trading software does not require additional hardware or software to be added to it.
Does the software require you to open multiple new windows when accessing different components or is it modular but contained within one window workspace?	This can be important as occasionally CFD traders mistakenly leave a hidden order window open and an error trade can sometimes result.
Does the trading software enable all open orders to be cancelled with a single click?	Some CFD providers have a 'panic button' in their software that enables a trader to quickly delete all open orders. This can be a very useful tool if markets are volatile.
What are the security aspects of the software? How easy is it to login and can passwords be saved?	If passwords can be saved to the computer then the software could be opened by someone other than the trader.
What are the procedures for cancelling an open order if the network connection fails or the provider has operational difficulties?	Can orders that are resting in the order book be manually cancelled via a help desk or some other means? No trader wants an open order that he can't cancel.
How is additional margin sent to the provider and what are the procedures for alerting a trader that he needs to top up his margin account?	Some CFD providers will send alerts via the trading software that a trader needs to place more margin into his account. This can be useful.
Can the trader change aspects of the trading software like fonts, alerts, colours, tones and brightness?	Traders often wish to customise their trading software and an easily customisable software program saves a lot of time.

Computing power and network connections

Most CFD providers offer guidelines regarding the technical specifications for computing power and network connectivity that enable CFD traders to successfully install and run their trading software. A good quality broadband service with a line of at least 1-2MB is normally preferable to a dial up modem service for its added bandwidth and reliability. The faster the broadband speed generally the better service will result.

These minimum PC guidelines are as follows:

Process	Range
CPU	300Mhz–2.5Ghz, Pentium 4
RAM	128-1024Mb RAM
Hard Drive	120-350Mb available space
Screen/resolution	1024 x 768 – 1280 x 1024
Colour	16 bit (65,536 colours) – 32 Bit (true colour)
Operating system	Microsoft Windows Vista, XP or 2000, Mac and LINUX

Mobile CFD trading access

Mobile trading in CFDs gives the CFD trader the opportunity to trade via a mobile Personal Digital Assistant (PDA) or a mobile phone using Windows CE operating system. The range of devices that can be used to trade CFDs is comprehensive, with most makes of mobile phone and PDAs acceptable; and the functionality for entering market orders, stops and limits orders is fully consistent with the types of order entry in the PC based trading software.

As device functionality and wireless Internet range and speed improves mobile trading will become more attractive to CFD traders.

Market data

Data services can vary significantly, with some data being generated by the CFD provider themselves and other data being provided through access to third parties. A typical CFD provider trading platform may have the following data sources:

- Live or delayed market price and trade data from exchanges, market makers or other third parties.

- Company news and corporate statistics from a third party like Bloomberg.

- General news and information from a third party news provider like Reuters or Dow Jones newswire.

- Live and historic customer account data, including margin levels, collateral in the form of available equity, and profit and loss profiles.

- Static data in the form of information relating to tradable instruments in searchable instrument trees, including contract specifications, symbols and subtitles.

The quality of market data that CFD customers interact with depends on the type of data service they adopt through their provider and their provider's ability to deploy that data. For example, UK CFD agent brokers will transmit market data in the form of SETS directly from the exchange, while CFD market makers provide market data based on the proprietary price quotations they are making.

Different trading instruments have different market data requirements depending on the level of their liquidity and the width of their dealing spreads. For example, banks may provide forex prices with very narrow dealing spreads directly from their price feeds, which speeds up transaction management. The demand for immediate access to deep pools of liquidity in forex requires fast, accurate market data services, whereas less liquid instruments (like some AIM stocks) will have wider dealing spreads and demand less in terms of immediacy with regard to data.

An optimal CFD trading set up

So far we have looked at CFD provider services at a minimum level. For those CFD traders who are looking for more sophisticated and higher level set-ups, there are additional things that can be done. The table below describes these additions.

Service	Comment
Two high quality **PCs** and two or more high quality **computer** screens	It is often optimal to use a separate PC for trading and one for everything else. Although PCs are more robust and powerful than they used to be, trading needs to be as fast as possible and a dedicated PC can help this. The non-trading PC can be used to access the Internet for email and chat rooms, research websites and so on.
Set up a **hot failover back up** for when the network connection goes down	Network outages can be very frustrating for a trader. It is optimal to have a second connection for trading as a hot failover from the primary network connection. This is not a cheap option but certainly an effective one.
Set up an audio **squawk box**	CFD traders cannot watch every move in a market but you can subscribe to a service whereby a continuous commentary is provided over an Internet connection from someone watching market events.
Use Excel for **recording trade data** and modelling trading strategies	Some CFD providers and data vendors have a DDE link from their trading software that enables a trader to download trade and price data real-time from the trading application to third party applications like Excel. This helps the trader to model strategies and play around with the data he receives.
Use an **independent data vendor** to provide real-time market data, analysis and prices in a range of instruments and companies	CFD provider data services are very good but they are not the sole business objective or service of the company. Data vendors like Reuters, Bloomberg, ESignal or Proquote provide enhanced services in this area.
Get as many **news sources** as possible	News sources are important and vary from broker services to CNBC and Sky news to Reuters. It all depends what markets a trader is trading in, but more news is always better.
Employ a **researcher**	Research assistants can be worth their weight in gold as an active CFD trader may not have time to research the companies or products he is trading in the detail he would like. Research assistants can be hired directly to work for the trader or their services can be used as and when necessary.

CFD trading software functionality

Creating workspaces

The primary objective for providers of online trading software is to enable their customers to easily and efficiently submit live orders and then to be able to manage those orders in a secure and robust environment, limiting undue risk and providing historical records of those transactions.

The various interdependent tasks associated with live online trading have prompted CFD providers to design trading software with a range of static or free-floating modules that can be pushed around the screen as potentially interlocking tickets and views that form a rigid montage. The various screen windows and views complement each other so that order entry, risk management, account management, and trade management components and tasks all work in unison in real-time. The modular design of trading software enables the user to customise their workspace, highlighting and selecting various modules and tools that they require to conduct their trading tasks, and positioning them into a view that they can lock. Once locked, the same view will appear every time they log into the trading application.

With regard to the construction of the trading software, customers select different components and functions to create customised workspaces. While the design and functions of the software can differ between providers, there are a number of generic tools and functions that all CFD trading software applications tend to have, such as the following:

1. pricing views

2. order tickets

3. instrument trees and search facilities

4. blotters

5. account management facilities

6. news and information views

7. charting tools

We will look at each of these in turn.

1. Pricing views

Pricing views enable customers to see live CFD prices as well as the prices of underlying market indices or other trading instruments. The views are customisable so that a range of different instruments can be selected via an instrument tree or search facility and displayed in one view. Columns that make up the view can be selected or deselected via a menu, and include:

- instrument symbol

- description of the instrument

- current bid-offer price

- high and low of the day

- net change in ticks or percentage

- volume traded

In some instances there is also a column highlighting the name of the market data provider.

Changes to the prices in each instrument are highlighted by a flashing colour so that if a price moves up, it is highlighted in blue, and if it falls it is highlighted in red. In some instances, a CFD provider may show a flashing colour if the instrument is subject to a sell or purchase order even if the price of the instrument does not change.

The pricing view is the window into the marketplace and therefore forms a vital component of the CFD trader's trading environment. Pricing views should have screens that are easy to navigate and tabs for quick selection of a range of different trading instruments, markets and tools. The views should provide access to several different trading instruments, including stocks, currencies, stock indices and index funds, should display information areas providing real-time market price data and streaming news items related to the traded instrument, and an order ticket. The market and price data should include several different instrument types and the following information:

- instrument symbol and description

- open position amount

- instrument bid and offer price

- tick box for highlighting if the open position should be traded out

The main areas of the graphical user interface (GUI) should be coordinated so that real-time changes in instrument prices are instantly reflected in the order ticket. Streaming news information means that announcements and general news relating to the instrument in question are relayed instantly. The GUI should be designed so that the CFD trader has all the information he needs in front of him in an easily digestible form, to be able to make quick decisions with regard to placing orders. The order ticket should be easily navigable giving the CFD trader the option to single click on the bid or offer in a defined quantity that is presented before trading. Because prices change rapidly, the view needs to convey instrument data very quickly, giving the CFD trader time to react by placing limit orders or hitting bids and offers.

2. Order tickets

Order tickets enable customers to view, send and modify orders in selected trading instruments in real-time. The information that is available needs to convey several things:

1. instrument,

2. type of order,

3. order quantity,

4. current bid-offer spread,

5. market depth of orders in the exchange central limit order book where available,

6. whether to sell or buy, and

7. whether to use a single click or a double click to send an order.

Order tickets have evolved from simply providing the opportunity to place market and limit orders to more complex views as a result of the increased sophistication of the order types that are now offered to customers. The objective is that they facilitate the speedy execution of orders in a user-friendly way while providing real-time updates in the CFD bid-offer spread.

3. Instrument trees and search facilities

Customers looking to trade on CFD trading platforms will need to search for tradable instruments from time to time via a database tree selection process, or via a search function similar to most Internet search engines. This information is known as static data, in that it is unlikely to change much over time. For example, if the stock symbol for Vodafone is VOD, the search facility should be able to instantly find it. This is unlikely to change in the future unless the company changes its name or status. Because of the large number of tradable instruments that CFD customers are able to trade, the tree search structure has proved to be the most efficient way to access tradable instruments in the database.

Instrument search

The speed and ease with which CFD traders can select new instruments in their trading GUI will often influence the outcome of their order entry speed, especially when markets are volatile and new opportunities present themselves in the rapidly changing prices of a range of instruments. In such markets, CFD traders need to search for different instruments quickly using a search facility or the drop down menu of different instrument headings. The instrument search tool is normally accessible from the main GUI. It enables the CFD trader to select multiple products quickly. Usually, trading instruments are ranked in alphabetical order under headings of the exchanges that list them or the category types that they fall under.

4. Blotters

Most CFD trading software packages provide a range of account information blotters that enable the CFD trader to view real-time order data, historic trade information, real-time account information including profit and loss, currency levels, transaction fees and interest payable or receivable. The objective of the blotter window is to provide real-time and historic account information quickly and efficiently so that CFD traders have access to current information to assist with their trading decisions. Again, ease of navigation and user-friendly functionality is a necessity in blotter windows, as the account information is a vital component to the trade decision-making process.

5. Account management facilities

Account management windows enable customers to view their real-time and historic account status in different currencies, their margin level and the profit and loss from their transactions collectively or broken down per trade, to deposit and withdraw funds from the account and to transfer funds between accounts.

6. News and information views

News and information modules provide real-time, or near-to real-time, data on a wide range of news topics or subjects. CFD providers normally have access to news providers like Reuters, Bloomberg and other streaming news providers directly through to the customer.

7. Charting tools

The quality of charting and technical analysis packages available to CFD traders varies from provider to provider. Most offer the basic charting functions, enabling customers to plot bar charts, line charts and candlestick charts of selected instruments with a range of technical analysis tools including moving averages, stochastics, Bollinger bands, relative strength indices and others.

More enterprising providers have extensive charting packages available to customers that enable them to plot their own trading positions into the price charting function and conduct 'what-if' scenarios with future price movements estimated for the instrument.

Charting has become a more sophisticated service over the previous few years, with charting tools providing what now amounts to a complete technical analysis system rather than just a simple view-only service. Reflecting the quality of subscription-level packages, some CFD providers offer customers high-quality charting systems enabling them to scrutinise historical data, modify data through drag and drop functions and to analyse patterns and trends that may form. In addition, the customer's own trades can be integrated into the charting tool so that they can see their open positions in the data range. Multiple instruments can be compared and contrasted, which lends itself well to trading strategy creation like pairs trading.

Placing an order

Sending a CFD order electronically via a CFD provider front-end trading system requires certain account, order type and product information to be included in the message. The information that accompanies the electronically generated order includes:

1. client account number,

2. which trading account the order is to be lodged in,

3. CFD contract that the trader wishes to deal in,

4. type of order,

5. whether it is a buy/sell or other strategy,

6. traded quantity,

7. price,

8. and any limitations on the order with regard to limits, stops or other conditions.

Orders can also be telephoned in to the CFD provider if necessary, although this process is not as quick as placing an order directly via an electronic system.

The mechanics of placing an order may differ between CFD providers depending on the trading software design. This section deals with practical order entry techniques and describes the following:

1. permitted order types

2. the process of sending a market order

1. Permitted order types

CFD order types range from simple market orders and limit orders to more complex multiple-legged orders that rely on several contingencies. This section describes the types of orders that CFD traders will come into contact with.

Order types are defined by the respective CFD provider. Usually the CFD order type reflects the same order type in the electronic exchange or marketplace so that CFDs are traded with conditions like limits, contingencies and stops in the same way as the underlying instrument would be.

A brief description of the main order types follows.

Market order

A CFD market order is an order type that requires filling immediately it reaches the CFD provider's electronic order matching engine. It stipulates whether it is a buy or sell and the quantity but does not stipulate a limit price at which to be filled.

There are two other types of market order; market on open (MOO) and market on close (MOC). The conditions of these order types stipulate that they should be sent to the marketplace electronic matching engine or market maker during the opening period or the closing period. Unfilled limit orders that are active during the normal trading session and have an MOC condition become market orders during the closing period.

Uses

Market orders are the most common order type used by CFD traders and are normally deployed in fast-moving markets where the transaction price is uncertain or the trader is keen to establish, or close, an open position as quickly as possible. Such orders are aggressive and are used primarily by CFD day traders and short-term traders.

Example

The BMW share price is showing higher levels of price volatility than usual ahead of its fourth quarter earnings statement. With two minutes to go before the announcement the CFD trader decides to take advantage of a sudden upward movement in the share price to buy 1000 CFDs at market. He believes that this jump in the share price is a result of the early release of the data to other market participants and is a signal that the earnings statement will be better than anticipated. He uses a market order because he does not want to be left behind if the BMW share price starts to rise quickly.

Limit order

A limit order has a price condition attached to it and stipulates a specific price at which it must be executed. So if I want buy Daimler AG at €33 (when the prevailing market price is €35), I will place an order to buy with a limit at €33. If the share price does not reach €33, my order will not be transacted.

Limit orders may remain unexecuted throughout the entire trading session and – depending on whether they are orders that are good for the day (GTD) or good until they are cancelled (GTC) – they may either be cancelled at the end of the trading session or will be extended into the next trading session.

Uses

Limit orders are often used to open new positions in CFDs where they provide some level of risk management, maintaining a specified price at which to enter the market compared to the immediacy of a market order. CFD traders may decide that the current share price is too high and elect to enter a limit order beneath the current price.

Example

A CFD trader is feeling bearish of the overall German market in the morning but is looking to buy Daimler AG on weakness at €32 below the current share price of €35. He enters a limit order at €32 and waits until the share price drops. By lunchtime the Daimler AG share price has only dropped to €32.50 so the trader increases his limit to €32.25 where he is more likely to be filled. Before the close the share price drops enough for the limit order to be activated and the order is filled.

As mentioned, limit orders can be entered good for the day (GTD) or good until cancelled (GTC) at the outset of the order being placed. GTD orders are cancelled at the end of the trading day if they are not filled, while GTC orders remain open during subsequent trading days until such a time as they are either modified, cancelled or they are filled.

Join bid and offer limits

Some CFD providers have developed functions in the order tickets in their front-end trading systems that enable CFD traders to enter orders to join the bid or offer price being quoted in the market.

Uses

Traders would use this kind of function to scalp trade in busy markets when the dealing spread between the bid and offer price often widens. That is, to place limit bids and limit offers into the order book in the expectation that the share price will fluctuate between the two prices enabling the trader to buy at the bid and sell at the offer.

This is a useful function which promotes active trading and aims to improve the entry and exit prices for traders. This function will appeal to active traders who rely on entering and exiting the market at short intervals in order to take advantage of price volatility. However, the trader must be careful to avoid being caught out by sudden breakouts in the share price on the upside or the downside that trigger his limit orders but propel him into immediate loss.

Example

In the following table the Porsche share bid and offer price is shown with corresponding bid volume and offer volume. The table shows that the offer volume is larger than the bid volume. A CFD trader decides to enter join limit bid and join limit offer orders in 5000 shares at 77.50 and 77.75 respectively in the expectation that he will be able to trade the bid-offer spread while the market is quiet. By buying at 77.50 on the bid and selling at 77.75 on the offer he will make €125 each time he transacts 5000 shares.

Bid volume	Bid	Offer	Offer volume
7000	77.50	77.75	23,000
10,000	77.25	78.00	7000
2000	77.00	78.25	120,000

However the CFD trader's order makes up a large percentage of the bid price volume and he is filled at his limit price by buying 5000 shares at 77.50 very quickly when the share price starts to fall suddenly.

As can be seen in the table below, the weight of offers following the falling share price pushes the bid price down to €76.00 before the trader has a chance to cover.

Bid Volume	Bid	Offer	Offer Volume
2000	76.00	76.25	3000
67,000	75.75	76.50	1000
2000	75.50	76.75	30,000

The trader was caught out by a small breakout in the share price and now has to decide what to do with his loss-making position.

Stop orders

A stop order is a purchase order with a price trigger that is above the current offer price or a sell order with a price trigger that is below the current bid price.

Using the same example as for the previous order (replicated in the following table)–

Bid volume	Bid	Offer	Offer volume
7000	77.50	77.75	23,000
10,000	77.25	78.00	7000
2000	77.00	78.25	120,000

A stop order could be entered to sell 5000 Porsche shares stop 76.00 or to buy 5000 shares stop 78.00. The stop order won't be triggered until the bid or offer prices reach the trigger levels.

Stop orders can be used to open new trading positions, close out open positions or reverse a position from long to short. A buy stop for example, can be used to create a new long open position above the current market price. The rationale for a trade of this kind is that the CFD trader may be watching for a stock to break through a resistance level above the current market price and may not be willing to take a long position before the price breaches this level.

Stop loss orders

Stop orders may limit the potential loss of an open long or short position (when they can be called stop loss orders), but they are not guaranteed to be executed at the price at which they have been set. In some cases, volatile markets cause gaps in share prices that fall through intended stop prices, and unless the stop has a limit price above or below which it will not be executed, there can be some slippage in the fill price of the order. The only disadvantage of entering a stop loss with a limit is if the price gaps down or up through the limit price and the order remains unfilled.

Guaranteed stop loss orders [described below] guarantee that a stop will be filled at a certain price.

Guaranteed stop loss or limited liability orders

The problem with stop orders is that they incur slippage if the market is moving very quickly. The trader may want to stop himself out of a long CFD position at a certain price below the current bid price in a fast falling market but the price can move very quickly and travel through his expected close out level. This is called slippage. There are two solutions to this problem: a stop limit, or a guaranteed stop. The stop limit offers no guarantees however and only part of an order may be filled if the market is moving very quickly.

In order to reduce the likelihood of price slippage with a stop loss order, a CFD trader can elect to open a guaranteed stop loss (GSL), or as it is sometimes called, a limited liability order.

A GSL order means that the CFD trader will be taken out of the position at exactly the stop price that he stipulates when it is reached whatever the circumstances of the market, so the CFD provider assumes the risk that there is a price gap in the instrument if the market becomes volatile.

As the GSL order dispenses with the risk of missing a stop loss price or the likelihood of excessive price slippage when a non-guaranteed stop order is being executed, there is a premium charge of between 0.75% and 1.00% for using the limited liability order type. The extra charge for placing an order of this type is levied before the order is placed.

CFD providers that allow the use of this order type also stipulate minimum incremental distances between the price of the GSL order and the current market price of the instrument. This means that some GSL orders may be placed 5-6% away from the current price of the underlying instrument.

In addition, CFD providers may only allow limited liability orders to be placed on blue-chip stocks with high levels of liquidity.

Trailing stops

A trailing stop has a special condition that enables the stop price to move up (if long) or down (if short) according to the movement of the underlying price. Trailing stops enable the CFD trader to take advantage of favourable price movements in an open long position, for example, by automatically raising the stop loss level every time the share price increases. A trailing stop level is set at a specified distance from the CFD price at the outset of the trade and will follow the share price up by that set amount. However, the stop price will not move down if the share price falls, thus locking in a profit margin.

Uses

A trailing stop is used by a trader when his open position is moving favourably into profit but he is concerned that a sudden downtick in the market may cause his profit to evaporate. In such circumstances, the trader places a trailing stop a few ticks away from the current share price so that it doesn't get activated too easily and rides out the noise in the market while expecting the share price to continue to move in his favour. Every €1 increase in the share price value will bring the trailing stop price higher by €1 in order to maintain its specific gap with the current share price.

Example

The trader has a long position of 10,000 shares at €72.00 and is expecting the Porsche share price to increase again over the next few hours. He wants to stay in his position as long as possible while the share price is rising but is mindful that the price may fall back below the current level at some point. He wants to make sure that he locks in some of the profit he has made so he places a trailing stop at €75.00, €1, or four ticks, away from the current bid price of €76.00. If the share price falls to €75.00 the trailing stop will be activated and the trader will sell his shares at a 'locked in' €3 profit.

Let's look at this in more detail.

The following table below shows a snapshot of the order book in Porsche with the best bid in the order book being €76.00 in 20,000 shares, and the best offer being €76.25 in 3000 shares. The trailing stop will be activated automatically if the bid price falls to €75.00 in which case the trader will sell 10,000 shares at that price.

Snapshot of the position of the trailing stop in the exchange's central limit order book

Bid Volume	Stock Bid	Stock Offer	Offer Volume
20,000	76.00	76.25	3000
67,000	75.75	76.50	1000
2000	75.50	76.75	30,000
30,000	75.00 (trailing stop at this price in 10,000 shares)	77.00	2300

Ten minutes later the share price falls to €75.00 and then lower to €73.00. The trailing stop was activated to sell 10,000 at €75.00 which means the trader receives his €3 profit and avoids the danger of losing more of his profit if the share price continues to fall.

One-cancels-the-other order (OCO)

With a One-cancels-the-other order type (OCO) if one of two orders is executed, the other outstanding order is immediately cancelled.

For example, a trader has an open long position in CFDs, and places a limit sell order above the current market price and a sell stop limit below the market price.

If the market price for the underlying goes up to the price set for the limit sell order, the long position makes a profit, and if the underlying price falls to the price set for the sell stop limit, the position makes a loss.

For example, if the share price is 45.10 bid and 45.30 offered the limit orders are placed at 44.90 and 45.50. If the price of the share falls to 44.90 and the sell stop limit order is filled, the corresponding sell limit above at 45.50 is immediately cancelled.

Once a CFD trader has established an open position in the market he will want to manage its risk and to cover the potential loss of an adverse movement in the CFD price, while at the same time exiting the open position at a given level above the current market price. Using trailing stops and OCO order types can provide a defined level of control that enables the trader to establish a trade and then to manage its profitability and risk.

Immediate or cancel, or 'fill or kill' orders

Market orders can have different parameters pre-loaded into their execution specifications. For example, if a market order is dispatched with an immediate or cancel (IOC) specification attached to it, it will trade at whatever price is available as long as the quantity matches the desired order quantity. If the trade cannot be transacted immediately in its entirety, the order is cancelled.

In the same way a 'fill or kill' order requires that the market order is filled in its entirety or cancelled.

The logic behind using these two order types is that the trader may not want to transact partial amounts of the order. For example, if a trader sends an order in 5000 CFDs and it trades only 100 CFDs because of the lack of volume on the bid or offer, then he will have failed in his trading objective and is left with a small open position in 100 CFDs only.

He may also have incurred minimum transaction commissions that make the transaction uneconomic.

2. The process of sending a market order

The process of sending an electronic market order to the CFD provider involves several issues. I will take each aspect at a time and explain the mechanisms involved.

Firstly, which trading screen enables the order to be sent and how is the order loaded?

Normally, the CFD trader's account details are saved and automatically loaded into the trading application once the trader has logged in. By saving the format of the workspace before he logs off the previous session, the trader can expect to see the same workspace configuration the next morning. With the trading account details in place, the trader can select the order entry ticket.

Preparing to enter an order

Before a CFD trader sends a market order he must do due diligence by checking the order parameters. Because a market order will trade as soon as it hits the marketplace, the trader needs to be certain that he has the correct information loaded. That is, he needs to check–

1. the **correct instrument** is loaded into the order entry window,

2. the bid and offer price corresponds to the **current price range** for the instrument,

3. the instrument is not in an **unexpected state** (e.g. auction or in a high state of volatility),

4. the prices are **live**,

5. he has loaded the correct **number of CFDs** to buy or sell,

6. that he is sending the order of choice (**buy or sell**), and

7. there are no **conditions** he needs to add to the order (e.g. limit or stop)

Are the prices firm?

The instrument bid and offer prices that are visible in the order ticket are normally firm, in that if there is available bid or offer volume, the market order should transact.

Sending the order: how do you click to trade?

If the trader is happy that he has the right parameters for the order, he can send the order to the market in a number of ways.

1. With some trading applications, he can use the **computer keyboard**. Although this is not the fastest way to send an electronic order it is still possible due to the use of hot keys that are pre-programmed to provide certain definable functions. For example, the instruction to 'send a market sell order' can be programmed into a key function on the keyboard.

2. The trader can **mouse click** with the cursor positioned on the bid or offer price on the order ticket. This function can be modified to accept a single or a double mouse click depending on the speed with which the trader wants to send the order. If the trader wants to review and confirm the order before he sends it with a single click of the order entry button on the order ticket, he would normally elect to have a double-click order entry function. On the second click of the mouse, the order is then dispatched.

How long does a market order take to transact?

Depending on the speed of the communications line into the CFD provider from the trading application, and the type of provider (broker or market maker) the order should transact within milliseconds. The execution price that the trader receives depends on the prevailing bid or offer price available at the moment the order hits the CFD provider's host matching engine or the market maker's desk. If the order price and size are consistent with the price and size of the quoted instrument, then the order should transact instantly.

How soon is the trader notified of the trade?

If the trading interface is responding in real-time to market orders and all of the parameters of the order are fulfilled, then the trade report should be received within milliseconds.

What happens if you make a mistake?

If the CFD trader makes a mistake, it is highly unlikely that he will be able to cancel the order unless there is some operational reason why it went wrong. Trading mistakes resulting in a loss that are no more than the result of a bad trading decision will not normally be revoked by the CFD provider. However, genuine errors that result from unforeseen functional or technical problems could be subject to change if the error was found not to be the fault of the trader.

4

CFD Trading Strategies

In this chapter we look at some of the main trading strategies used by CFD traders, why they are used, how the strategies are structured and what risks they assume. Once the CFD trader has a thorough knowledge of the trading strategies to deploy during certain market conditions, the intra- and inter-day market movements become more recognisable and strategies can be viewed as part of a trading plan rather than as a reaction to isolated events.

Wide use of a mature product

The product characteristics of CFDs mean that they are suitable for a number of trading strategies and have, over the last ten years, become mainstream trading instruments. Their strength lies in their versatility, with uses ranging from speculation through leverage, short selling opportunities, risk offset of cash positions, portfolio capital management and corporate event trading.

CFDs are not subject to time limits but, as described in a previous chapter, there is a point when holding a long CFD becomes more expensive than holding the cash stock. As such, most traders use them for either short to medium term speculation, or for the hedging of physical stock portfolios.

It should be remembered that markets are not efficient and that not all information about a stock, bond or other traded instrument is available to all traders at the same time. Neither is it fully reflected in an efficient price for that instrument. Opportunities are everywhere, as long as the CFD trader can execute trading strategies quickly and efficiently.

Chapter structure

The first section of the chapter describes the methods behind establishing a trading plan. Every CFD trader should have one before they start trading.

The second section deals with the following trading strategies:

- Speculative trading strategies

    - long CFD

    - short CFD

    - opening auctions

    - market momentum/pyramiding

    - scalping

- Market neutral trading strategies

    - pairs trading

- Special situation trading strategies

    - index re-weightings

    - rights issues

- Portfolio risk management

    - hedging

The following table summarises some of the characteristics of these strategies.

Trading strategy summary table

Strategy Type	Description	Strategy Objective	CFD User Benefit	Strategy Users
Speculative				
Long CFD	Net long CFD	Go long CFDs looking for favourable upward-moving instrument prices	Leveraged long profit opportunities	Retail, proprietary, smaller hedge fund
Short CFD	Net short CFD	Short position using favourable stock borrowing and financing arrangements on CFDs	Leveraged short profit opportunities	Retail, proprietary, smaller hedge fund
Event driven	Net short or long CFD	Gear short or long position using favourable financing arrangements on CFDs to corporate events	Dividend event financing benefits for long CFD holders	Hedge funds, asset managers, retail, proprietary traders
Market momentum	Net short or long CFD	Pyramid short or long position to leverage momentum trades	Leveraged profit opportunities	Hedge funds, asset managers, retail, proprietary traders
Short-term trading	Scalping by trading the bid-offer spread	To buy on the bid and sell on the offer	Low cost trading strategy	Retail, proprietary, smaller hedge fund
Market Neutral				
Pairs trading	Long and short relative value trade	Capitalising on changes to the relative spread differential between two related products	Easy to deploy, no stock borrowing requirement, mirrors cash market, low cost	Hedge funds, asset managers, retail, proprietary
Special Situation				
Index re-weighting	Net long market instrument Short index CFDs	To profit from the increase in share price in a stock that is due to enter an index	Long (short) stock, short (long) index CFD creates a market neutral strategy	Hedge funds, asset managers, retail, proprietary
Portfolio Risk Management				
Balancing a portfolio using a short-term hedge	Full hedge with short CFD	Short-term risk management using CFDs	Easy to deploy, mirrors cash market, low cost	Hedge funds, asset managers, retail, proprietary

Developing a successful trading approach

Establishing a trading plan

One of the most important elements of successful trading is to have a trading plan. Without a well structured plan, a CFD trader will be prone to making ill-considered choices with regard to trade entry and exit points, poor judgement with regard to the way in which market information is portrayed, erratic choice of the types of strategies that could be deployed and the tendency to be subject to decision-making biases that adversely affect trading profitability. Building a trading plan takes time and knowledge, and the CFD trader must be careful to incorporate an element of flexibility should market conditions change abruptly.

It is important to acknowledge and understand which type of market participant you are, and to establish a trading plan that reflects the parameters within which you can operate. A CFD trader must decide what he or she is looking to achieve with regard to their activities in the market. As outlined, this will, in part, be determined by the prevailing market conditions, but will also be a function of the trader's level of acceptable risk and capital requirements. Understanding the prevailing market conditions requires access to information and market knowledge.

Example trading plan

The following describes a trading plan for a CFD trader who is expecting to take advantage of short-term volatility in the European pharmaceuticals sector. The trading plan has the following components:

1. a clear overall trading objective

2. preliminary preparation required

3. a trading plan and trading methods

4. clearly defined risk parameters

The main objective of establishing a trading plan is to leave very little to chance. Preliminary research and preparation can take weeks but it very rarely gets wasted when the trader starts to trade in live markets. By understanding the stocks and their movements implicitly, nothing is left to chance.

Overall trading objective

To trade for a three-month minimum period between January 2009 and April 2009 in the stock CFDs of four European pharmaceutical companies.

To increase the current trading capital amount of €100,000 by 20% over this period without incurring losses of more than 10% of the trading capital available at any one time.

Preliminary preparation

Select four European pharmaceutical companies that have high market capitalisation, (above €5bn) high trading liquidity in the bid and offer prices shown on the exchange electronic order books, and are featured in the DAX 30, FTSE 100 or CAC40 indices.

Corporate information

Gain full understanding of important corporate dates and events of each stock including AGMs, earnings announcements, dividends announcements, ex-dividend dates and pay dates, capital raising endeavours like rights issues and placings and officers of the company including CEO, CFO, CTO and other notables.

Understand each company's status within the industry and their relationship with their peers, whether they are potential bid targets or bidders, what notable research is being undertaken and which drug patents are due to be lost or gained.

Find out who the largest shareholders of each company are and whether they actively trade in the company's stock.

Find out when the directors of the company last dealt in the company's stock, what their transactions were and if there are any significant changes in director's shareholdings.

Trading information

Understand the logistics of the share price movements of each company, including trade tick sizes and values, sector index weightings and larger index weightings. Observe how the share prices move intra-day and inter-day and make notes on the types of transactions that take place including recurring trades with similar sizes, trades that seek to sweep the order book, and any large volume distinctive trades that occur.

Estimate how many other market participants are trading at particular time intervals during the day and what types of transactions they perform. Note if their trading behaviour moves the share price one way or another.

Make notes of any distinct algorithmic trading activity, what it seeks to achieve and when it occurs.

Observe and note which macro economic statistics affect the share prices, how and over what time intervals.

Observe and note the typical intra-day highs and lows of share price movements. For example, if the normal daily high/low range is 20 ticks then this has an impact on where stop loss levels are placed.

Determine the average historical intra-day volatility of each stock and where the current volatility level is.

Trading plan	Trading method
To maximise short-term profit potential through intra-day long and short directional trading positions in CFDs.	To open long and short CFD trades when the stock prices move at least 0.5% above the previous night's closing price and show signs of sustained momentum. To open short CFD trades when the stock prices move at least 0.5% below the previous night's closing price and show signs of sustained momentum.
To limit overall losses to 10% of the trading capital available and to cease trading if this level is reached.	Employ the use of stop loss limits at no less than 10 tick intervals away from the prevailing share price. As the typical intraday trading range of each stock is no more than 15 ticks, this limit level will be unlikely to trade unless the stock breaks out significantly and the position moves into extreme loss. However, the open position is in danger of being stopped out if the interval is too close to the prevailing share price.
To use the trading capital in a measured way	To open long and short CFD trades using no more than 30% of the available trading capital in each CFD trade, and with no more than three open CFD long or short positions using 10% of the available capital at any one time.
To maximise profitability through intra-day trading exposure to the volatile ranging price movements of the stocks	To scalp trade placing bids and offers simultaneously at the top of each side of the order book, but with no more than 5% of the available capital in each trade.

Choosing strategies

The trading plan and the types of CFD trading strategies to use are determined by the following:

1. the overall trading objective

2. the historical and current market conditions

3. the degree of acceptable risk

4. the levels of available capital and cost of financing

Once the CFD trader has developed the trading plan on the basis of his research findings, he should build an armoury of trading strategies for different market scenarios, and must be versatile and quick enough to deploy them without hesitation when the opportunity arises. There are a group of well-known CFD trading strategies that are used in various market conditions. They include:

- Short-term, aggressive, speculative trading strategies using long and short positions to take advantage of spikes in market volatility and abrupt price movements.

- Strategies that capitalise on the changing price differentials between products (often referred to as market neutral trades).

- Strategies that profit from special situations such as takeovers.

- Risk management and hedging strategies.

- Exotic strategies that combine CFDs with cash and derivatives.

It is also imperative that the trader has good sources of market information available to him, the more information the better as some novice CFD traders rarely use more than one piece of information to confirm when to open new long or short positions. Believing in a single, isolated instance of confirmation, where several may be needed to verify a particular strategic stance, can lead to higher than reasonable levels of confidence, which conversely increases the frequency of loss-making trades.

A measured approach to trading using historical and real-time market information is to look for several instances of confirmation, including:

- Current news and views on the traded instrument from professional analytical sources.

- A fair value assessment of the price of the instrument relative to its historical average.

- Technical analysis of the preceding days, weeks and months of price movements in the stock.

- Knowledge of when special reports or corporate events are likely to be announced, including dividends, commodity supply reports, directors' dealings and earnings.

- The relative performance of the instrument to other instruments in the same sector.

- Any special situations that could, or are, influencing the price of the trading instrument, including forthcoming dividend adjustments to the share price due at the ex-dividend date, the terms of corporate mergers and acquisitions, and broker's reports.

Avoiding poor decision-making

Novice CFD traders have a tendency to match their preconceived ideas and strategies to the market rather than assessing the market and creating strategies based on its expected movements. Those traders with an unsubstantiated bullish or bearish bias wait for market rises or falls beyond what could be termed the action/reaction point; that is, the point before which a decision should have been made to open a new position, a point when the market was unmistakably rising or falling.

After the action/reaction point has passed, it is likely to be too late to enter the market with a new open position in the hope of making a profit. In short-term bullish scenarios, the average action/reaction spectrum can be as short as 5 or 6 seconds. That is, the time decay period during which a potential trade starts to lose its appeal and changes from being a positive selection to a potentially negative one. CFD traders who have a firmly rooted, but unsubstantiated, bullish bias tend to require only a single instance of confirmation for their strategy before entering the market with a new open position, and this can prove to be fatal.

Market conditions

Market conditions are in a constant state of change throughout the trading day, but there are some acknowledged and easily identifiable active and quiet spots in most markets. For example, in the European securities markets, trading activity can be influenced to varying degrees by the following (that tend to occur at regular intervals):

- Market opening and closing times

- Pre- and post-market auctions

- The set time for announcing macro economic statistics

- Corporate statements, AGMs, profit & loss statements, and interim and final results

- Dividend announcements

- Lunchtimes

- The opening times of other markets and how they influence the domestic market

- Derivative market expirations and how they affect the cash markets

CFD traders should be aware at the point during the trading day at which certain influences occur. In addition, an understanding of the changes in the volume of traded business accompanying these times is important.

Dealing with abrupt changes in prices: bids and takeovers

Abrupt and unexpected changes in market sentiment causing irregular and sharp price movements can immediately derail a trading day. Sudden changes in the directional movement of a market or trading instrument can spell disaster for a CFD trader who has not had a chance to close open CFD limit positions above or below the market level.

Some CFD traders use a method of speculation whereby they stack limit bids and offers above and below the current market best bid and offer (BBO) at different tick increments, hoping to capitalise on short-term price movements away from the BBO that then revert to the average price or the mean.

For example, if a CFD BBO is 330-33 on a stock, CFD traders often place limit bids at 329, 328, 327 and 326, and offers at similar price intervals above the offer price to capture any short-term blips up or down in the price. The expectation is that any short-term blips will soon rectify themselves by returning to the BBO 330-33 level promptly, thus making trades at beneath or above the market profitable. The CFD trader must, however, be careful not to leave too many limit bids and offers in the market should a sudden price move activate them before the trader has a chance to delete them.

Breakout scenarios

Sudden breakouts provide traders with very good trading opportunities, but they are difficult to anticipate. A CFD trader is unlikely to make money consistently if he or she tries to 'call the turn' in the share price and could experience several loss-making trades

Experienced CFD traders learn and adapt. Continual exposure to varied market conditions creates additional learned responses and over time, traders become more aware that certain market scenarios are playing out with particular market conditions. The degree to which a trader has the ability to repeat previously successful and profitable behaviour while trading in market scenarios that are similar or the same as those he has encountered before, ultimately determines his long-term level of success. Equally, the way in which a trader is able to automate profitable performance will influence his overall trading success.

Ultimately, traders should try to automate as much of their successful trading behaviour as possible through the use of automated scripts and programs, if not merely to reduce the more mundane order entry tasks they undertake in their trading activity. A simple example of this would be the use of trailing stops. Traders invariably forget to put stops in play when they are most needed, or tamper with them when they are in place. An automated tool that places trailing stops in the market following the opening up of new positions is a very useful addition to a trader's arsenal of tools. Through an accurate understanding of their trading behaviour, traders will be able to automate many more of their trading functions, leaving them time to concentrate on other aspects of trading, including analytics and strategy creation.

Sideways-moving markets

Markets don't always experience prolonged periods of volatility. They can have extended times during which very little happens and the prices of traded instruments tend to move in a sideways direction. This can prove to be difficult and frustrating for CFD traders, in that the benefit of leverage is best deployed in markets that are experiencing directional momentum. The CFD trader needs to have a plan of action for times when the markets are quiet. During these periods, which can be intra-day or longer, the main objective of the CFD trader is capital protection. Capital can be eroded gradually when it is difficult to see trends developing in markets.

Trending markets

Upward or downward trending markets are likely to form the basis for most profitable CFD speculative trading. If a trading instrument has adopted a price trend in a particular direction, the best strategy that a trader can deploy is to join it. The leveraged opportunity that CFD traders have, as well as the lack of stock borrowing and favourable financing arrangements, means that they can fully capitalise on trending markets by holding positions for extended periods of time or adding to them as they become more profitable. This is known as pyramiding.

Level of acceptable risk

There is a general belief in trading that no single trading position should amount to risk exposure of more than 5% of a trader's available capital. Although this is not set in stone, it is a practice that many traders use. Most traders acknowledge that they are likely to lose more often than they win, but what is important is to make the winning trades more profitable and to cut the losing trades faster. Given that a CFD trader is subject to positive and negative leverage, if he or she deploys more than 5% of allocated trading capital to one trade and the trade goes into loss, the momentum with which the trade loses money may increase dramatically, thus prompting the trader to deliver more capital in the form of additional margin to their provider. If the trader does not deal with losing trades in a ruthless manner, by cutting them quickly and decisively, then capital can be eroded very quickly.

Although stop losses can be established, it is notoriously difficult to pick the right distance away from the current traded price to place the stop, and losses can accumulate due to the incidental triggering of stop loss limits when markets are volatile. In all, it is very easy to lose money if the CFD trader does not have a pre-determined risk threshold and a firm understanding of the limits for each trade.

Choosing the best trading approach and trading instrument

Before I go on to describe each of the trading strategies, I want to briefly consider the difficulties some CFD traders have in picking the right instrument to trade. CFD traders often have difficulty picking underlying instruments that suit their temperaments, trading styles and personalities. It is likely that they will find their niche product through the experience of trying out several different products in real-time markets, as simulated markets are unlikely to create the right risk-based scenarios for them. Spending time experimenting with trading products can be a laborious and costly undertaking, but one that up to now has been unavoidable.

In addition, one of the hardest tasks for a CFD trader is to know where to set entry and exit points for a given trading strategy. For example, should a CFD trader use technical analysis in order to establish support and resistance levels and then place orders at these points, or should the trader look at the dynamics of the market and judge (through observations of the order flow) where reasonable entry and exit points are? Traders can find it extremely difficult to judge the right point to join and leave the market, and many rely on judgment calls to place their orders. Without a firm idea of whether a trade has been transacted or exited at the right point, successful trading can be elusive.

CFD traders need to consider very carefully the types of products they wish to trade, especially when they are starting out for the first time. While new traders are getting used to online trading for the first time, it is advisable that the products traded should include some of the following qualities.

1. Liquid trading volume

The regular level of traded volume must be taken into consideration by new CFD traders, as more liquid instruments tend to create the opportunity to enter or exit a position without unduly influencing the price of the instrument. If liquidity is always present and bid-offer spreads are tight, then CFD traders are more likely to be able to exit poor positions without undue difficulty. As new CFD traders become more confident trading in liquid markets they can then consider trading less liquid markets that may respond more readily to their trades.

2. Recognisable price movements and behaviour

The 'per tick' incremental size of the product is also important, because lower incremental tick sizes are less likely to create exaggerated position risk. In addition, products with lower incremental tick sizes have lower exposure to irregular market moves. Exaggerated market moves will obviously create greater risk for products with lower tick values, as they would for products with higher tick values, but the lower the per tick value, the less likely traders are to blow up too rapidly.

3. Identifiable fundamentals

For new CFD traders it is useful to be able to identify the major influences on a trading instrument, be they, for example, crop yield figures, corporate actions, level of interest rates, housing starts or FX levels. The more influences on a trading product that the trader knows about, the better able he or she will be to maximise the potential for profit while controlling risks associated with the product.

4. Ready access to data

It is also important to have access to as much data associated with the product as possible. Electronic markets need transparency and the trader must be as informed as possible at all times. Price data also provides the CFD trader with the basis for strategy evaluation and historical analysis of their trading plans.

5. Establishing your 'banker'

It is not unusual for new CFD traders to spend a year experimenting with different trading products. The objective is to locate a traded instrument that the CFD trader clicks with, gets to know extremely well and feels very comfortable trading. The 'banker' is the traded instrument that the CFD trader can turn to in times of market turmoil and which will provide him with his daily bread. In terms of a stock, the CFD trader understands his 'banker' with regard to the dynamics of its price movements, its normal and abnormal levels of traded volume, the corporation behind the stock, and its corporate event dates, including dividend dates and interim and final results, the historical price behaviour of the stock and any market influences that affect the price.

Central limit order book behaviour to be aware of

There are subtleties that the CFD trader should be aware of with regard to using DMA to SETS Level II. Although the limit order book appears to be transparent to the trader, all may not be as it seems.

Delayed trade reporting

The market depth of bids and offers that show the volume of trades that are pending transaction at prices above or beneath the current best bid and offer can be misleading. There are reporting rules that permit a delay in reporting large off-book trades, which, if they were to have been transacted on SETS would have impacted the level of the order book.

Spoof orders

Professional traders utilise a number of trade execution and order management techniques to achieve an advantage in the limit order book, and can spoof the market with illusory bids and offers in an effort to flush out institutional order flow and latent stop loss or limit orders.

There are examples of professional traders loading up bids or offers a few ticks away from the best bid-offer spread, giving the impression to other traders that the market is well supported or offered. This, in turn, prompts other traders to join bids or offers in the mistaken view that there is real business at these prices. Then, when the loaded bid or offer order gets close to a price where it will be transacted, it is swiftly withdrawn, leaving other traders exposed. The spoof trader then turns the table on the other traders and takes the bids or offers they are showing. This is sometimes known as *flipping*. A bid or offer price may look to be well supported, when all of a sudden substantial order size disappears from view leaving those bids and offers remaining vulnerable to execution.

Trying to read the bid and offer volume is an art in itself, and some professional traders make a living from it. For CFD traders, it is always worth bearing in mind that spoof orders exist and to treat order volume and liquidity with caution.

The second section of this chapter describes different trading strategies that CFD traders use.

Speculative trading strategies

Long CFD

Description

A long CFD strategy is normally undertaken when a CFD trader expects the underlying traded instrument to rise in price. When a trader believes that a stock index, such as the Swiss Market Index (SMI), is going to rise in price, he buys index tracking CFDs on the SMI.

Example

A trader buys 5 index tracking CFDs at the prevailing SMI price level of 7450. He is able to leverage €2000 by 20 times with his CFD provider, because the provider only requires 5% margin on index CFDs (as they are historically less volatile than individual stocks). He holds the open position for 10 days, during which time the index rises to 7585, and he sells the 5 CFDs for a 135 point profit.

This trade is summarised in the following table.

Trade summary table

	Trader: Long Swiss Market Index (SMI) (CHF)
Day 1	
Customer margin	2000
Cost of 5 index CFDs	37,250
Commission charged at 0.15%	(56)
Day 10	
Closing notional transaction value	37,925
Commission charged at 0.15%	(57)
Financing charge at 1.5% above CHF LIBOR (2.5%)	4% x 37,250 x 10/360 = (41.38)
Profit before deductions	675
Total profit after deductions	520.62
% return on equity	26%

Strategy notes

The CFD trader was able to take a highly leveraged position in the index without having to commit a large amount of capital.

Short CFD

Description

CFDs provide the opportunity to go short of a traded instrument, like a stock, without having to borrow stock to deliver. In the cash UK market, delivery of a short stock has to be undertaken by T+3, that is, on the third day after the trade was undertaken. This can present a challenge for traders and institutions alike, as the short stock will have to be borrowed from a broker, which will incur stock lending costs. These costs range from 10-40 basis points and can represent a significant proportion of the expected profitability of the trading strategy. Selling short CFDs not only creates leverage, but also dispenses with the challenges of borrowing stock to cover the short position. In fact, the short CFD position attracts a financing *credit*.

The power of leverage with CFDs, as opposed to the difficulties that short stock sellers can experience, can be seen in the following example where there are two traders, one that sells stocks and the other CFDs. They each decide to take short positions in Persimmon.

Example

Client A decides to place a short stock trade in Persimmon PLC for 25 days and has talked to his Prime Broker who has had difficulty arranging for stock to be lent for a period in excess of eight days before which the shares need to be delivered. In this instance, the short selling institution has two choices:

1. To close out the short position within eight days to avoid settlement, or

2. To incur additional costs by rolling over the short position for a further 17 days to meet the target expectations of the strategy.

As the client has a premier relationship with his broker, he has an option to leverage his cash deposit of £50,000 by up to 3 times. This means that the overall capital at his disposal is £150,000. The broker charges a commission of 0.25% and the client decides to go ahead with his strategy, selling 19,736 Persimmon PLC shares at the prevailing bid price of £7.60.

Client B also has £50,000 available, this time to lodge as margin in order to engage in the same short trade in Persimmon PLC. The CFD provider allocates Client B 10 times leverage, so that the notional value of the available capital is £500,000. Client B sells 65,789 Persimmon PLC shares at £7.60.

Short stock positive

- Client A is able to benefit from his Prime Broker relationship by using 3 times gearing.

- Client A does not have to worry about counterparty risk with the CFD provider.

Short CFD positive

- The short CFDs offer higher leverage opportunities than the short cash position and therefore better potential profit margins.

- Client B will attract a financing credit with his short CFD position.

- Client B is not required to lodge the notional value of the total short position of 65,789 shares.

During the 25 day period, Client A rolled over his short stock position, which added to his costs as he was charged additional commission and stamp duty. Client B maintained his short CFD position and benefited not only from the drop in the share price of Persimmon over this period of time, but was also credited with interest in his margin account at 1%, that is 1.5% below LIBID (2.5%). Client A and B both closed out their short positions on the 25th day showing a profit, with the share price 25p lower at £7.35.

Trade summary table

	Client A: Short Persimmon PLC stock (£)	Client B: Short Persimmon PLC CFDs (£)
Day 1		
Customer equity/margin	50,000	50,000
Notional transaction value at 3x (stock) and 10x (CFD)	150,000	500,000
Commission charged at 0.25%	(375)	(1250)
Stamp duty	-	-
Day 8 rollover		
Stamp duty (0.5%)	(750)	-
Commission charged at 0.25%	(375)	-
Day 25		
Closing notional transaction value	145,059	483,549
Profit before deductions/interest	4941	16,451
Commission charged at 0.25%	(362.65)	(1208.87)
Total income through finance interest	-	500,000 x 1%
Stamp duty (0.5%)	(725.30)	-
Net profit	2353.05	14,339.13
% return on equity	4.7%	28.7%

Strategy notes

- The percentage return on equity for the short CFD position outstrips the return on the short stock position by a significant amount.

- The short CFD position attracted a financing credit, while the rollover costs of the short stock position eroded £1000 of the potential profit due to stamp duty on the purchased shares and the commission payable.

- Although both traders anticipated the right move in the stock, the CFD trader was better able to capitalise on it.

- The short CFD position would have incurred large losses had the stock price in Persimmon increased rather than decreased.

Pyramiding

Description

Deploying a series of long or short leveraged trading strategies that result in profitable speculation is not an easy thing to achieve. Repeating profit-making success over time in different market scenarios is even harder. Although speculation can yield handsome profits for those CFD traders who get their directional play right, there are several factors that CFD traders need to be aware of when taking leveraged long and short positions in order to avoid loss. Perhaps the most important is to recognise that gearing works in a speculator's favour or to his detriment in equal ways. A technique to manage geared exposure is pyramiding positions.

With market momentum strategies, the CFD trader is encouraged to add to winning positions as the trend establishes, rather than to place all available capital into a long trade at the outset of a move.

Example

A CFD trader has recognised that a stock, Tesco, is trading in a short-term, upward trend. Over a two-day period between 11 and 12 July 2007, the stock price rose consistently in an upward moving channel from a low of £4.12 on the morning of 11 July, to a high just above £4.30 at the close of business on 12 July. This 18 point movement represented a strong trend, and the CFD trader spotted it at £4.18 on the morning of the 11th, when the strength of the stock meant that it had breached its previous daily high and refused to drop down below £4.17. The trader opened a long CFD trade in 5000 CFDs at £4.18. However, he waited until the stock price had shown strength at £4.22 on the morning of 12 July to add another long position in 5000 CFDs, pyramiding his open position and increasing his profit. During the day, the stock price remained above £4.25, showing signs of support. As the US market opened strongly in New York at 2.30pm BST, the CFD trader added an additional 5000 CFDs to his position at £4.25, and established a stop loss at £4.23 and a target exit point at £4.30.

The CFD trader exited his long 15,000 CFD position when the share price temporarily broke through £4.30 just before the close of business on 12 July.

Trade summary table

Day 1–11th July 8.00am	
Share price	£4.18
Action	Buy 5000 Tesco CFDs
Notional transaction value	£20,900
Commission charged at 0.25%	(52.25)
Stamp duty	0
Day 2–12th July 8.00am	
Share price	£4.22
Action	Buy 5000 Tesco CFDs
Total trade position	Long 10,000 CFDs
Notional transaction value	£21,100
Commission charge	(52.75)
Day 2–12th July 2.30pm	
Share price	£4.25
Action	Buy 5000 Tesco CFDs, set stop loss limit for 15,000 at £4.23, set target exit point for strategy at £4.30
Total trade position	Long 15,000 CFDs
Notional transaction value	£21,250
Commission charge	(53.13)
Day 2–12th July 4.15pm	
Share price	£4.30
Action	Sell 15,000 Tesco CFDs at £4.30
Total trade position	Flat
Total notional transaction value	£64,500
Commission charge	(161.25)
Total transaction profit	1250 – (319.38) = £930.62

Strategy notes

- The CFD trader pyramided his positions by adding 5000 CFDs at intervals without taking undue risk of opening up a preliminary large long position of 15,000 on the morning of 11 July.

- This enabled him to reassure himself that the upward trend was gaining momentum and that it would be potentially profitable to increase his long positions.

Scalping: bid-offer spread capture

Short-term trading opportunities arise when market volatility increases, because the increased risk that volatility creates tends to widen bid-offer spreads in most instruments. CFD traders can take advantage by scalping between the wider spread differential while the market remains directionless.

Description

Scalping is a trading method that takes advantage of the trading volume at the bid and offer price of an instrument. If, under normal market circumstances, a commodity such as wheat has best bid and offer prices of £6.34-6.36, with a standard 2 pence spread, then the scalper must look to establish long positions at, or below, the bid price, and short positions at, or above, the offer price.

He achieves this by effectively market making in the instrument, sending limit bids into the market at £6.34 and limit offers into the market at £6.36. By sitting on the bid and the offer, the CFD trader is hoping to capture sellers and buyers simultaneously, thus taking small regular 2 pence profits.

This method of trading becomes more profitable the wider the instrument's bid-offer spread becomes, so with sudden increases in market volatility, the CFD trader is ready to reduce the prices on his limit bids and offers in order to match or improve the best bid and offer on the suddenly widening spread. As long as the market remains volatile but directionless, the scalper is able to capitalise on the price swings between the bid and offer.

Scalping positives

- CFD traders can position trades into the market price depth of the instrument with the expectation that there will be sellers and buyers either side of the best bid–offer spread.

- If the price remains range-bound then scalping can be a very lucrative trading strategy.

Scalping negatives

- Scalping profitability will be harmed if resting limit bids and offers become subject to fills when the price breaks out of its narrow, directionless pattern.

- The CFD trader can find himself either short in an upward moving market or long in a downward market.

- Scalpers risk being caught out in sudden breakouts, and the leverage created by CFD positions amplifies losses if the losing positions are not closed out quickly enough.

Market-neutral trading strategies

Pairs trading

Description

Stocks whose prices are historically correlated, particularly those within the same sector, can experience unexpected divergences in the ratio of their prices, so that traders can take advantage of the divergence of relative values of those stocks while they remain out of kilter. Pairs trading involves selling a temporarily overpriced instrument and buying an underpriced instrument both of which have a historically close price correlation.

For example, if the Barclays Bank share price is underpriced and out of line with the Lloyds TSB price, a CFD trader would buy Barclays Bank and sell Lloyds TSB.

The objective with a pairs trade is to capture the price ratio retracement of a large price move in a stock relative to another. For example, a trader can open a long or short position in a stock with a related stock in the same sector or industry, and profit from the retracement. In addition, large moves in sectors can see some constituents of the sector move more rapidly than others. Being prepared to go short or long one stock against another can be a rewarding strategy. It is not always necessary to trade stock pairs in the same sector or industry.

If a CFD trader believes that one stock is under-priced compared to another, then he can buy the cheaper stock while selling the more expensive one. While this strategy reduces overall exposure to market movements as the trade is established on a cash neutral basis, it enables the trader to capitalise on short-term misalignments in the two share prices.

What are the risks involved?

Open positions in two previously correlated stocks can quite suddenly become seriously offside for no apparent reason. No matter how closely correlated the prices of two stocks may have been historically, those correlations break down from time to time.

It is also worth remembering that with CFDs, the short position is not subject to stock lending requirements. This means that CFD traders who engage in pairs trades are not in danger of having stock called away from them, or subject to costs related with stock lending. In addition, the short stock leg of the CFD strategy attracts a financing credit.

Example

A CFD trader believes that the stock prices of BP and Royal Dutch Shell have temporarily moved out of line. Traditionally closely correlated, the gap between the share prices of both stocks has widened, suggesting that Royal Dutch Shell is overpriced compared to BP. The trader lodges margin at the level of 10% of the aggregate value of the total contract consideration.

The trader buys 10,000 BP CFDs at £5.625 and sells 3099 Royal Dutch Shell B CFDs at £18.15 so that the aggregate market position is cash neutral. The price ratio is 3.22 (18.15/5.625). The trader holds the position for 4 days, during which time the spread between the two stock prices narrows to a price ratio of 3.12 (17.90/5.725).

Trade summary table

	Long BP PLC CFDs (£)	Aggregate	Short Royal Dutch Shell B CFDs (£)
Day 1			
Notional value of each open position	56,250	112,500	56,250
Aggregate margin level at 10%		11,250	
Commission charged at 0.2%		(225)	
Day 4 – trader closes position			
Financing cost/credit of aggregate open position at 1% above LIBOR (4%) and 1% below LIBID (3.75%)	5% x 56,250 x 4/360 = (31.25)	17.19 – 31.25 = (14.06)	2.75% x 56,250 x 4/360 = 17.19
Notional value of each open position	57,250	112,722	55,472
Commission charged at 0.2%		(225.4)	
Profit before costs	1000	1778	778
Total profit after costs		1313.54	
% return on equity		11.7%	

Strategy notes

- The pairs trade has worked well with the ratio of the BP share price to the Shell share price narrowing

- A strategy of this kind can also be risky as correlations can break down temporarily between share prices

Opening auctions

Description

Between 7.50am and 8.00am, the London Stock Exchange engages in its pre-market auction. During this short period of time, stock orders are entered into the central limit order book, SETS. The equilibrium opening price is established at the open of the trading day (around 8.00am) by weighting the buy orders versus the sell orders at particular prices. The Exchange's objective is to match as many orders and as large a volume of business as possible at a single price at the open, so the matching algorithm seeks to establish a balanced opening price that is a fair weighted average of all those orders that are entered.

The following table shows a random group of incoming orders that are ranked by the algorithm.

Range of incoming orders in Barclays Bank PLC pre-market open

Limit bids in Barclays Bank PLC	Limit offers in Barclays Bank PLC
Buy 1000 at 5.00	Sell 50,000 at 5.06
Buy 50,000 at 5.00	Sell 50,000 at 5.08
Buy 10,000 at 4.90	Sell 250,000 at 5.00
Buy 1000 at 4.96	Sell 1000 at 4.96
Buy 25,000 at 5.00	Sell 2000 at 5.05
Buy 4500 at 4.99	Sell 4500 at 5.07

All of the incoming stock limit orders, both buy and sell, are graded according to their price and size forming a mixture of orders at different levels. The Exchange electronic algorithm ranks them by giving those orders with larger size a weighting advantage. In this case (as illustrated in the preceding table), although there are more sell orders in the £5.05-5.08 level, the Barclays opening price might be closer to £5.00, as the only sizable order of 250,000 is at that price. In addition, there are 76,000 shares at the limit bid of £5.00, so it is highly likely that the opening price will be £5.00 as the greatest number of shares can be traded at that level.

As well as limit orders, the pre-market order book also holds market orders, and these are immediately transacted at the opening price, which adds to liquidity.

Occasionally, stocks that are historically correlated can see temporary divergences in their prices, so that traders can take advantage of the mismatch in relative values of those stocks until they regain their equilibrium.

Although the ratio of instrument stock prices is continually changing (and forms the basis for a well-known trading strategy called pairs trading) the opening auction presents a definable opportunity brought about by an event that happens every day. Traders can sometimes make their day's trading profits during the first 10 minutes of the pre-auction trading day in this way.

Example

At the previous night's close the ratio of the Barclays Bank and Royal Bank of Scotland share prices was 1.07:1 (£5.00/£4.67). During the opening auction indications are that the ratio is now 1.14:1 (£5.06/£4.44). The Barclays share price is temporarily inflated because of an imbalance of incoming purchase orders versus sell orders, and the RBS share price is lower because of a negative broker's report.

The trader expects the ratio of the two stocks to balance at 1.09 (£4.98/£4.57) within an hour of the opening bell, so he sends an order to sell 10,000 CFDs in Barclays Bank at £5.04, and an order to buy 10,000 CFDs in Royal Bank of Scotland at £4.47. This will establish a ratio of 1:12:1, and will create a profit of 16 ticks if he is correct.

By 9.17am the Barclays price is £5.02 and the RBS price is £4.61. The stock ratio is 1.089:1 and the CFD trader has made 2 ticks on his short Barclays position and 14 ticks on his long Royal Bank of Scotland position.

Trade summary table

	Short Barclays Bank PLC CFDs (£)	Long Royal Bank of Scotland PLC CFDs (£)
Trader equity	5040	4470
Notional transaction value 10x (CFD)	50,400	44,700
Commission charged at 0.25%	(126)	(111.75)
Stamp duty	-	-
Closing notional transaction value	50,200	46,100
Commission charged at 0.25%	(125.5)	(115.25)
Profit/loss before deductions	200	1400
Total profit/loss	(51.5)	1173

Strategy notes

- The overall profit from the transaction is £1121.5, which as a percentage return on equity is 11.78%.

- The pairs correlation ratio has not resumed its previous day's level of 1.07:1, but has drifted towards it, thus proving the trader right in his assumptions.

- Had the CFD trader traded stocks instead of CFDs, and kept the open position for longer than a day, then he would have incurred stamp duty (in the UK) on the day following the transaction when he closed his position. The CFD position, however, would not have incurred the 0.5% stamp charge.

Special situation trading strategies

Index re-weighting

Fund managers whose funds' performance are expected to match a stock index will buy stocks that enter the indices and sell stocks ejected from the indices after the announcement has been made, in order to retain the correct weighting of portfolio stocks in relation to the index. CFD traders can take advantage of the buying or selling demand that this situation creates.

Example

The Morgan Stanley Capital International (MSCI) indices are capitalisation-weighted, and therefore stocks that reach a certain level of market capitalisation are considered for entry. There is an annual review of the indices in May, with an announcement on the new constituents entering the index at mid-month, with the index adjustments being made at the end of May. Fund managers will seek to rebalance their portfolios during the period between the announcement and the actual adjustments, so as to keep them correlated with the new index make-up.

If we take the example of Bovis PLC being added to the MSCI United Kingdom Index in 2005, we can see the opportunity for profit during the announcement time and the gap of two weeks before the stock joined the index. The Bovis PLC share price moved from £6.29 to £6.84 between 12 May 2005 and 31 May 2005 (a rise of just under 9%).

The strategy that could have been deployed to take advantage of this price movement was to go long of Bovis CFDs and short an equivalent value of FTSE 100 CFDs. The short FTSE 100 CFDs neutralises the market risk of the stock position.

Trade summary table

	Long Bovis CFD (£)	Short FTSE 100 CFDs (£)
12 May	Stock price 6.29	Index level 4893
Action	Buy 10,000 CFDs at 6.29	Sell 13 CFDs at 4893
Notional value of each open position	62,900	63,609
Margin level at 5%	3145	3180
Commission charged at 0.2%	(125.8)	(127.20)
Stamp duty	0	0
31 May (trader closes position)	Share Price 6.84 (£)	Index level 4964
Action	Sell 10,000 CFDs at 6.84	Buy 13 CFDs at 4964
Notional value of each open position	68,400	64,532
Financing rates	1% above LIBOR (4%) = 5%	1% below LIBID (3.75%) = 2.75%
Financing charges (£)	68,400 x 5% (19/360) = (180.5)	64,532 x 2.75% x (19/360) = 93.66
Commission charged at 0.2%	(136.8)	(129)
Profit/loss before costs	5500	(923)
Total profit/loss after costs	5056.9	(1085.54)
Total strategy profit	**3971.36**	

Note: Financing costs used in this example are an approximation as they are normally calculated overnight based on each end-of-day notional value using actual daily rates.

Strategy notes

- The short FTSE 100 CFDs made a loss, but created a market neutral strategy limiting the market risk to the strategy.

- Including Bovis in the MSCI (UK) Index was very positive for the share price.

Rights issues

Rights issues can present good trading opportunities for CFD traders, as:

1. The market volatility of a stock normally increases when it announces a rights issue.

2. When the rights shares are tradable on the market as nil paid shares, they are often priced at a lower price to the main share price. This can add volatility as they are continuously brought into line with the ordinary share price through arbitrage and spread trading. They are often traded as one of the legs of a pairs trade with the ordinary share.

3. If the ordinary share price dips below the rights issue share price then the nil paid shares effectively become penny shares that behave like at-the-money options with an effective strike price at the rights price and consisting of only time value. That is, value based on the likelihood that the nil paid rights will go 'in-the-money' sometime before they go fully paid in a month's time.

Example

A rights issue that will serve as a good example is the HBOS rights issue which was announced on 22 April 2008; the offer was: two rights shares for every five shares currently held. This means that if a shareholder has 2000 shares they are entitled to buy a further 800 shares through the rights issue giving them a total of 2800 shares.

When the HBOS rights were announced the share price immediately fell from around £5 to under £4.20. With the average value of the shares ex-rights being under £4.35, shareholders were able to see what the company believed its own true value to be. In this example with HBOS, the market took it badly and the share price dropped consistently for several weeks until it went below the level of the rights price.

This presented a good trading opportunity with the nil paid rights increasing and decreasing 40-100% in price in volatile trading days.

Trade summary table

Day 1 8.05am	
Nil paid rights share price	£0.09p
Underlying share price	£2.89
Rights issue level	£2.80
Action	Buy 10,000 nil paid rights CFDs
Total trade position	Long 10,000 CFDs
Total notional transaction value	£900
Commission charge at 0.25%	(22.5)
Day 1 12.34pm	
Nil paid rights share price	£0.14p
Underlying share price	£2.94
Rights issue level	£2.80
Action	Sell 10,000 nil paid rights CFDs
Total notional transaction value	£1400
Commission charge at 0.25%	(35)
Total profit	£442.5 (£500 - 57.5)

Strategy notes

- For CFD traders rights issues increase volatility of the stock on an intra-day basis thus giving rise to opportunities to trade increased volatility. For example, when news emerged that RBS was preparing to launch a rights issue, increased volatility hit the share price with a daily swing of up to 8%.

Portfolio risk management

Hedging

Traders who have portfolios of shares may wish to prevent a fall in their value by using a method known as hedging. Hedging is a technique used to control the risk of holding a long position in an instrument or a portfolio by taking an equal and opposite position to the long position by going short another instrument, whose price movements are correlated. CFDs are effective instruments for hedging as described below.

Example

A CFD trader has held long positions in Volkswagen, Porsche and Daimler AG for six months during which time the stocks have appreciated by nearly 10%. He is concerned that their value may fall in the short term after two brokers recently issued profits warnings. Although the short-term picture may be less promising, the CFD trader does not want to sell the shares as he is expecting a recovery in the share prices after a short-term fall. The portfolio holds 1000 shares of Daimler AG and Porsche and 200 shares of Volkswagen.

Rather than sell the shares (and incur significant costs) the CFD trader decides to hedge the portfolio by selling CFDs for three weeks.

At the end of the three week period, the value of the portfolio overall has fallen by nearly 8%.

Summary of trades

	Portfolio	Short Daimler CFD (€)	Short Volkswagen CFD (€)	Short Porsche CFD (€)
Day 1				
Share price		33	269	70
Action Long	1000 Daimler AG, Long 200 VOW, Long 1000 Porsche	Sell 1000 CFDs	Sell 200 CFDs	Sell 1000 CFDs
Notional Transaction Value	156,800	33,000	53,800	70,000
Commission Charged at 0.25%		(82.50)	(134.50)	(175.00)
Stamp Duty		0	0	0
Day 21				
Share price		31	248	65
Action		Buy 1000 CFDs	Buy 200 CFDs	Buy 1000 CFDs
Notional Transaction Value	145,600	31,000	49,600	65,000
Commission Charged at 0.25%		(77.50)	(124.00)	(162.50)
Financing credit of open short CFDs at 1% below LIBID (3.75%)		2.75% x 31,000 x 21/360 = 49.73	2.75% x 49,600 x 21/360 = 79.57	2.75% x 65,000 x 21/360 = 104.27
Loss on Portfolio	-11,200			
Profit on short CFDs plus finance income minus Commissions		2000 -77.50 - 82.50 + 49.73 = 1889.73	4200 -124.00 - 134.50 + 79.57 = 4021.07	5000 - 162.50 - 172.50 + 104.27 = 4769.27
Total hedge position (loss)	-11,200 + 1889.73 + 4021.07 + 4769.27 = -519.93			

Short CFD positive

- The short CFDs effectively hedged the portfolio.

- The stock holder is able to leverage cheaply and provide a direct hedge to his stock portfolio without having to sell it.

Strategy notes

- During the 21-day period, the portfolio falls in value by 11,200 euros. The stockholder realises a loss on his stock portfolio that is offset by 95.4% by the profit on his short CFD positions. The imperfect hedge is due to commission charges.

5

CFD Regulation

Regulation

Background

CFDs are a classic example of a financial product created in response to a specific regulatory constraint, therefore they need to be understood in the context of their regulatory environment. As off-exchange derivatives, they were originally viewed as institutional trading instruments and attracted limited regulatory oversight due to the professional status of the counterparties trading them.

Regulators believed that if experienced financial institutions were dealing with each other then CFD issuers and their professional counterparties should understand the product risk profile without requiring heavy regulatory control and oversight. However, as CFD trading became more widespread in the 1990s and began to attract less sophisticated retail investors, the need for regulatory control became more pronounced.

In the 1990s the problem for regulators was to determine how light a touch they should exert on CFDs while protecting investor interests without stifling a fledgling global market with excellent prospects for future growth.

Original benefits

The original benefits of trading CFDs, aided by benign regulation, were clear: in the UK for example, the avoidance of UK Government stamp duty, leveraged short selling opportunities without the need to engage in stock borrowing and, up until recently, the ability to influence corporate governance through covert equity stake building and partial avoidance of FSA Disclosure rules affecting normal stock and options purchases.

Elsewhere, in Europe and Australia, the attractions of CFDs do not include Government stamp duty relief but all other benefits, such as leverage, short selling and wide choice of trading instrument are present.

However, now that extreme leveraged trading and short selling have been highlighted as possible influences in the destabilisation of global financial markets, the favourable regulatory status for CFDs has been challenged.

Global regulators have issued statements about CFDs, notably in June 2007 in the FSA's November CFD Directive, and have undertaken research into them to understand if they pose a true threat to market stability.

It is true to say that since the creation of CFDs in the UK in the 1980s they have presented global market regulators with a number of challenges. By understanding their original trading purpose during this time we can understand their current regulatory footprint more easily.

In this chapter we will look at the following topics as they relate to CFDs:

- global efforts to control financial market instability and how CFDs factor into this
- global regulation of CFDs
- the pan-European regulatory environment for CFDs
- CFD best execution and price discovery
- short selling rules and CFDs
- the UK FSA disclosure regime and the effect of CFDs on corporate governance
- European Union rules for money managers and fund managers
- European fund management UCITS rules allowing funds to trade CFDs

Global regulation of CFDs

Although rules relating to CFD regulation may differ between countries, the continuing effort of global regulators and finance ministers to contain recent financial market instability has been universal.

Efforts on the part of regulators, for example, to control the deluge of short selling that markets experienced in the US and Europe in the summer and Autumn of 2008 and the first quarter of 2009 were mirrored in Asia and the Middle East shortly after short selling controls were put into place by the US SEC and the UK FSA.

The Japanese finance regulators opted on 28 October to bring forward restrictions on short selling Japanese stocks following marked declines in stock values when the Nikkei 225 Index lost over 18% of its value over a 5-day period.

MiFID and the Pan European Regulatory Environment for CFDs

MiFID

Launched on 1 November 2007, the overall aim of the European Markets in Financial Instruments Directive (MiFID) was to increase competition and to establish better rules for investor protection. Through its wide-ranging changes to European financial markets legislation, MiFID ushered in a new era of competition between market centres which has created fragmentation of the European Equity marketplace by removing previously restrictive 'concentration rules'.

Pre-MiFID, such rules required equity trades, for example, to be executed on exchanges, or contract markets, like Deutsche Boerse, Euronext or the London Stock Exchange, but MiFID legislation – which opened the door to new alternative trading venues known as Market Transaction Facilities (MTFs) – caused an increase in the number of Alternative Trading Systems (ATS) to enter the marketplace – like Chi-X, BATS and Project Turquoise – that compete for the same trading business as the more established exchanges.

The fear is that with more MTFs likely to enter the marketplace, UK and European equity markets will form fragmented liquidity pools rather than create the basis for a homogenous pool of liquidity over a short time period.

Aggregation requirements

Direct Market Access CFD providers faced a challenging initial task when the MiFID was introduced in 2007 in that they were required to provide access to new market centres in order to aggregate best bid and offer prices in European equities and to order route to the market centre offering the best executable price. Previous to MiFID they could offer price dissemination and order routing to a single marketplace.

CFD price discovery

CFD traders rely on the accurate representation of the underlying instrument best bid and offer price through the CFD price they receive from their brokers, so that they can deal at the same prices broadcast at the exchange or marketplace. This is important as it upholds the credibility of the derivative OTC CFD market based on the underlying cash market and forms the basis of Direct Market Access (DMA).

CFD market makers, who make their own dealing spreads, also rely on the accuracy of the underlying instrument price in order to set their own prices. They are sensitive to any changes in the conditions of the underlying instrument be they price, liquidity or status.

It should follow, then, that CFD traders can expect to have their orders filled at prices that are deemed to be the most efficient and are accurate representations of the market. This, after all, is the basis of the central limit order book, on LSE SETS for example, where the bid-offer spread represents the tension between incoming purchase and sale orders.

CFD providers are obliged to pass on the benefits of the deep liquidity inherent in the central limit order book to their clients, and the FSA, through MiFID, ensures this.

CFD best execution

MiFID recognises that there are many issues that influence the best execution quality of a client order that may not be readily apparent to the customer. These factors include:

- Order type
- Size of the order
- Settlement arrangements and the timing of the order
- Cost of executing the order with regard to explicit costs that the CFD provider charges the client
- Implicit costs when a particular order moves the market price itself. In addition, there is the opportunity cost of not dealing at all.

The focus of MiFID, and in particular Article 21, with regard to the best execution policy is that the CFD provider must achieve best execution for a customer based upon wider criteria than price alone, and that they must regularly monitor the effectiveness of their execution policy.

This will mean that CFD providers are required to establish a formal best execution policy and provide regular reports as to the effectiveness and performance of that policy.

So, CFD providers must abide by Article 21 by disclosing their best execution policy and their order execution policy.

Such a policy is likely to include:

- An explanation of the way in which the **firm's prices** for financial spread bets and CFDs are constructed, including details of the charges applied by the firm to the price of the underlying (the benchmark reference price).

- An explanation of how the **price of the underlying** is determined, including confirmation that the firm seeks to identify the best possible result on a consistent basis for the underlying financial instruments (irrespective of whether the firm actually acquires the underlying financial instruments).

- Details of the **financing charges** that are applied for margined positions.

- Other information to enable the client to check and confirm the **pricing calculations**.

CFD market makers will also be obliged to match, or improve upon, best executable prices elsewhere in the marketplace, or to route orders directly to those markets quoting the best price if they themselves are not able to provide a spread that matches or improves upon the market's best dealing spread.

Market makers will be able to route orders to other transaction points seamlessly through the use of smart order routing – a technology that has been around for several years. Using this state-of-the-art technology, the objective will be for the CFD provider to check the best executable prices with several marketplaces before providing the CFD customer with a readily executable quotation.

What does MiFID's legislation mean for CFD traders?

CFD traders can look forward to benefiting from the advantages of a larger liquidity pool of European cash instruments once the issue of fragmented sources of price information is solved.

In the meantime, however, CFD traders and DMA providers are finding that they are presented with a multiplicity of market liquidity pools, which potentially makes the task of choosing which one to trade with quite difficult.

Some market participants, particularly equity and CFD brokers, complain that it is difficult to guarantee best bid and offer prices for their clients because of the fragmentation of trading venues.

Consolidated price data services

In January 2009 a group of Europe's alternative share trading platforms formed an alliance to discuss the creation of a new data service that provides a consolidated view of share prices offered across all of Europe's markets. This is a direct assault on the control exchanges like Euronext, Deutsche Boerse and the LSE currently have over selling share price data.

The challenge is further complicated because brokers can report their trades to places other than the exchanges, like BOAT, again fragmenting services and increasing the number of data sources available to market participants.

The US experience: European CFDs and their regulation in the US

CFDs currently have no formal legal definition in the US but under the umbrella of 'investment contracts based on the performance of equity securities', are currently viewed as 'securities' by the US Securities Act of 1933.

CFDs also fall within the definition of single stock futures which are under the regulatory control of the Commodity Futures Trading Commission (CFTC).

Subsequently due to legal restrictions in place for foreign stock trading in the US, European equity CFDs will not be offered to US domiciled traders until the US regulators offer foreign single stock futures in their domestic markets. Also, given the current turmoil in cash markets in the US, and the view of many US legislators that CFDs are risky trading products, it is unlikely that legislation will be changed in the near future to accommodate their inclusion into the trading mainstream in the US.

Short selling rules and CFDs

Stock borrowing and short selling CFDs

Short selling has long been considered a legitimate market activity. The FSA believes that short selling, when undertaken in a responsible manner, has a positive contribution to make to the operation of efficient markets under normal market conditions.

Nevertheless, the FSA has said that if future short selling creates a threat to orderly markets it will be prepared to reintroduce the short selling ban which it removed in January 2009.

Stock borrowing

Under normal circumstances stock borrowing is undertaken by brokers to facilitate client CFD orders, but may be limited if the underlying instrument is hard to borrow. A short seller of a cash equity instrument must borrow that instrument in order to satisfy the delivery after T+3.

If there is limited borrowing opportunity in a stock because, say, it is subject to a takeover, a rights offering or other corporate event, then there is a risk that a short CFD may be recalled.

In some instances when a stock becomes difficult to borrow, margin requirements for trading CFDs can be raised near to 100%.

Is short selling destabilising?

With regard to short selling, the degree of leveraged shorting that institutions and individuals trading CFDs can enjoy is now, following research undertaken by global market regulators, believed to be potentially destabilising to markets, especially during times of high volatility.

Aggressively speculative trading behaviour, demonstrated by hedge funds and trading professionals during extreme market conditions related to falling stock values, has put pressure on the global regulators to exert better regulatory control over short selling related to vulnerable stock sectors like banks, financial companies and property companies.

The catastrophic falls in banking sector stock prices, for example, in the summer and autumn of 2008, and the apparent speculative selling frenzy associated with the collapse in the stock values of Lehman Brothers and Bear Stearns prior to their demise, has been strongly criticised.

To what degree speculative short selling of CFDs can be blamed for exaggerated share price falls is difficult to tell, but the ease with which short selling was undertaken in cash equities and CFDS during this period prompted the FSA, and other global regulators, to ban short selling either entirely or in certain vulnerable stock sectors.

New short selling regulations

The FSA banned the short selling of 29 leading financial stocks including the banks on 19 Sep 2008 (this ban was lifted in January 2009). The SEC banned short selling in 799 US financial institutions on the same day, and the Australian market regulator banned short selling of Australian securities on 23 Sep 2008.

Under the new UK rules investors who have taken a short position have until 3:30p.m. the following business day to disclose it. However, they are only required to disclose the initial short position.

In addition, the negative impact of short selling on the success of corporate rights issues has been targeted by the FSA. The HBOS and RBS rights issues in April 2008 attracted a substantial level of short selling bringing the banks share prices well below their ex rights prices within the life of the rights issues.

After funds declared their short positions on 23 June 2008 it was evident that many of them had taken significant short positions in the rights issues currently underway.

The RBS offer of 11 shares for 18 shares held, at a price of 200p, already represented a 46% discount to the closing share price the Monday before its announcement. By the time the rights issue had failed two months later, even after being further discounted to 65.5p per share, the RBS share price had plummeted to 54p, a fall of over 80% from its 380p level 12 months earlier.

Investors now need to reveal any short positions over 0.25 percent in companies going through rights issues.

The FSA has concluded that a lack of transparency of short positions might leave investors unable to see the extent to which short selling might be influencing the price of a stock.

It also suggests that some level of transparency may be appropriate to help investors understand the factors driving trading in particular stocks. This could help the market understand if a stock is overvalued, so creating greater pricing efficiency.

FSA disclosure regime and corporate governance

The FSA believes that CFD use on an undisclosed basis to build up large equity stakes in takeover target companies in a bid to influence their governance could create potential market failures.

Until November 2007 FSA framework required disclosures of actual stock holdings and stock options where they represented over 3% of the shares of the company (and where they go over each percentage point thereafter). CFD positions did not have to be disclosed under these rules.

Since November 2005, the Takeover Panel has separately required disclosure during offer periods of CFDs and other derivatives of 1% or more in the securities of a target company.

The FSA believes that non-disclosure creates:

- inefficient price formation,

- a distorted market for corporate takeovers; and

- diminished market confidence.

So from November 2007 investors are required to disclose holdings of more than 3% in any one company in a combination of CFDs and shares. 3% was the level at which holdings of shares alone had to be disclosed prior to this date.

The FSA rejected its initial preferred option which was to have provided a safe harbour from disclosure. It was believed that this 'safe harbour' approach would have created too many loopholes which could have undermined the regime.

The FSA put together a consultative paper following which it decided that CFD holders will have to declare interests – comprising CFDs and shares – of 3%, the threshold originally set for shares in the Companies Act of 1985. The only exemption will be CFD writers who hold long CFD positions as a result of writing short positions for clients.

Below is a table of regulations and legislation including a content summary that provided the FSA with its framework for making a decision concerning disclosure rules.

UK FSA Regulatory Framework for CFDs	Content summary
UK Company Act 1985	The Act under which the Department of Trade and Industry oversaw the UK's major shareholding regime before handing over responsibility to the FSA on 2007. The Act brought within its scope contracts and other arrangements, such as call options, warrants and other types of options that enabled a person to acquire or to exercise control over the rights conferred on a shareholder.
European Commission's Financial Services Action Plan (FSAP)	The overall objective of the FSAP is to promote the competitiveness of the European economy. Sufficient transparency and disclosure are seen as key preconditions to liquid and efficient markets that, in turn, should lower the cost of capital for companies and deliver benefits for investors.
Transparency Directive (TD) (Formerly controlled by the Department of Trade and Industry)	FSMA section 89A(3)(b), together with 89F(1)(c), gives FSA powers to extend transparency rules to include instruments with a similar economic effect to financial instruments that give a legal entitlement to acquire shares (i.e. CFDs).
Disclosure and Transparency Rules (DTR)	CFD positions may be subject to disclosure under the DTRs if CFD holders have formal or contractual rights to exercise voting rights, or acquire underlying shares.
City Code on Takeovers and Mergers' (Takeover Code)	Has required the disclosure of economic interests in large shareholdings in certain circumstances
Market Abuse Directive (MAD), July 2005	The FSA Code of Market Conduct, sets out the types of behaviour which could constitute market abuse under the terms of the MAD. This includes (Market Abuse Rules 1.8.1): 'the dissemination of information by any means which gives, or is likely to give, a false or misleading impression as to a [qualifying investment] by a person who knew or could be reasonably expected to have known that the information was false or misleading.'
Financial Services and Markets Act 2000	The Principles for Businesses set out in the FSA Handbook apply to authorised persons. For example, the FSA would regard any authorised firm misrepresenting its position as potentially failing to conduct its business with integrity and/or not observing proper standards of market conduct.
Takeover Panel's disclosure rules (November 2005)	The Panel rules now require that if, during an offer period, a person directly or indirectly has an interest, including an economic interest, in 1% or more of any class of relevant securities of an offer or of the offeree company, or as a result of any transaction will have an interest in 1% or more, then all dealings in any relevant securities of that company by that person (or any other person through whom the interest is derived) must be publicly disclosed.

UCITS

In 1985 The European UCITS Directive (The Undertaking for Collective Investments in Transferable Securities) laid out certain minimum requirements for funds, prohibiting investment in certain types of riskier assets and setting out maximum levels of investment in, for example, the paper of one issuer.

Since 1985, the rules have been tweaked slightly. The range of financial instruments that may be invested in via UCITS now includes:

*   transferable securities and money market instruments

*   bank deposits

*   units of other investment funds.

*   financial derivative instruments

*   index tracking funds.

The definition of transferable securities is:

*   shares in companies and other securities equivalent to shares in companies;

*   bonds and other forms of securitised debt; and

*   any other negotiable securities which carry the right to acquire any such transferable securities by subscription or exchange.

UCITS 3

In December 2001, the third generation of UCITS (UCITS 3) enabled a UCITS fund to partially invest in derivatives or instruments of economic interest like CFDs by permitting it to invest an overall combined limit of 35% of its assets in the following investments:

*   transferable securities and money market instruments;

*   deposits; and/or

*   derivative instruments

The importance of UCITS 3 is that it enables portfolio managers who normally engage in long only investments the opportunity to include short positions to the portfolio through the use of listed and over-the-counter derivatives for more than simple hedging purposes which includes CFDs.

This enables fund managers to introduce greater flexibility and choice when constructing and managing their portfolios. However, with greater flexibility come a number of important restrictions.

European fund managers of long-only funds can now engage in selling short via derivatives for the first time in order to capitalise on falling share prices. Previous to this legislative change, they were only able to capitalise on stock price weakness by being underweight in targeted stocks but were precluded from using any form of derivative to short stocks. Now they can engage in what are called 130:30 funds where 30% of the portfolio, namely the weaker stocks, can be shorted, using CFDs for example. This strategy has the effect of retaining a portfolio with a net long position of 100% but theoretically enjoys enhanced profit potential through targeted short positions.

Furthermore, they must be able to demonstrate that they have sufficient risk controls to monitor exposure to the above instruments, including the ability to monitor OTC derivative exposure to each counterparty; and they must not have more than 10% of fund NAV exposed to any single counterparty in OTC products.

6

The Future of CFDs

What is the future for CFDs?

The rise in popularity of CFD trading has coincided with, and could be argued to be a direct result of, revolutionary developments in the ways in which financial markets operate – particularly for the semi-professional and retail customer.

Using an online trading platform, traders are able to access an array of order management and trade execution services that are designed to enhance the user experience and promote efficient trading.

For the first time in financial markets history, many individual retail and semi professional traders are considering safeguarding their own financial futures rather than leaving their capital in the hands of money managers who charge sometimes upwards of 1% of the notional value of the fund per annum as a management charge.

As a result, these traders now want greater control over the way they manage risk, more dynamic trading instruments, transparency in markets, and effective trading and analytical tools.

Electronic trading has enabled the non-professional trader to share the domain of the professional and to achieve a much broader spectrum of investments – the true hedge for any trader.

Should CCP replace OTC?

Off-exchange trading: non-exchange listed CFDs

Another area of interest for the future that must be considered is the fact that OTC CFD transactions are not undertaken on a recognised or designated investment exchange. The risks to the trader associated with this fact are as follows.

- While CFD providers who offer DMA for listed exchange products will match the bid-offer spreads on those products throughout the exchange's official trading hours, they also offer out of market hours trading when there is no officially listed price. This means that the trader is trading at an OTC price that has no immediate reference to the price of the underlying instrument. Although the flexibility to trade outside of exchange official trading hours can be an advantage to some CFD traders, the price the OTC provider offers may be very different from the opening price on the exchange once official trading begins.

- If the provider is an OTC market maker, then the trading price will reflect the bid-offer spread that they create and, as such, the CFD trader will trade with them directly. This means that the OTC market maker has control over the spread and may decide to widen it at any time, thus making the prospect of hitting bids or taking offers more costly.

- In addition, all CFD trades that have been opened with a particular OTC provider must be closed with them, as there is no designated exchange with an accompanying central clearing counterparty (CCP) to close out positions with.

- In some cases, it may not be possible to close an open position with an OTC market maker or broker to determine the value of an open position if there is no tradable reference price, especially if the product is listed on an exchange and has been suspended.

- Lastly, the OTC CFD provider themselves also pose a risk with regard to the solvency of the company. For example, there is a risk that the CFD provider may default if capital adequacy levels become strained.

Exchange listed CFDs

Exchange traded CFDs (already listed by the Australian Stock Exchange) are different to listed CFDs in that they may soon be available to be traded through the central limit order book (CLOB), whereas listed CFDs are provided by a single market maker.

Innovation

The challenge for CFD providers will be to continue to innovate as CFDs become a mature product. Now that leveraged trading opportunities are available through other derivative products, such as spread bets, traders are scrutinising CFD provider fee structures, interest payment schedules, overnight funding charges, the width of dealing spreads and other characteristics of the CFD marketplace. Whether or not CFDs will remain the instrument of choice for many traders and traders depends upon the ability of the CFD providers to offer greater value.

As part of the financial market's innovation, the appeal of CFDs is likely to continue as long as taxable benefits remain in place and regulatory organisations like the FSA allow their use. Also, with greater numbers of traders joining the marketplace to take advantage of higher levels of market volatility, the use of CFDs as a speculative trading product is likely to expand.

Fundamentally, CFDs provide an alternative liquidity pool to the market of a cash instrument, be it liquid or illiquid, in its own right. As such, the opportunities for its use will continue to expand as new initiatives, like exchange traded CFDs, push the product further into the investing mainstream.

Index

'banker' 127

A

account segregation 86

accounts

  advisory 76-77

  discretionary 76

  execution only 76

  limited risk 77

action/reaction 121

alternative trading systems (ATS) 155

B

BBO, see 'best bid and offer'

behaviour

  patterns 123

best bid and offer (BBO) 122-123, 127, 135, 155, 156, 158

best execution 16, 74, 154, 156-157

bias 16, 74, 154, 156-157

bid-offer spread, see 'spread'

blotters 93, 97

C

capital adjustments 60

capital gains tax (CGT) 5, 11, 13, 31, 54, 63

cash v, 3, 25, 27, 58, 171

central clearing counterparty (CCP) x, 12, 29, 30, 169-170

central limit order book, see 'order book'

CFD

  account opening 69-72

  agent broker 14, 81

  charges 4, 35, 45, 48, 71

commission 45-47

  definition 3

  exchange listed 11, 170

  exchange traded 170

  funding ix, 35, 52-53

  hedge 16-17, 147-149

  listed 11, 170

  long 6-7, 52-53, 62, 129-130

  non-exchange listed 169-170

  provider 69-72

  short 7-8, 48-49, 62, 130-132, 149

  stock 38-39

  trading software 87-89

CGT, see 'capital gains tax'

Charting Tool 97-98

charting, see 'technical analysis'

click to trade 109

collateral 4, 5, 42, 83, 86, 91

commodity vi, 9, 10, 24, 28

company news 91

company research 71

compulsory closure 82

computer requirements 90

corporate actions 60-66, 118, 121

correlation 22, 23, 80

costs

  financing 10, 11, 22, 35, 48-54

counterparty 10, 11, 15, 22, 35, 48-54

    risk 29-30

currency pair 53

customer

  contact 84-85

  types of

    institutional vii, viii, ix, 5, 45, 80

    intermediate 73, 74-75, 76-77